IMAGES OF WAR

The Hawker Hunter

IMAGES OF WAR

The Hawker Hunter

RARE PHOTOGRAPHS FROM WARTIME ARCHIVES

MARTIN W. BOWMAN

Pen & Sword
AVIATION

First published in Great Britain in 2020 by
Pen & Sword Aviation
an imprint of
Pen & Sword Books Ltd
Yorkshire – Philadelphia

ISBN 978 1 52670 560 0

Typeset in 12/14.5 Gill Sans by
Aura Technology and Software Services, India

Printed and bound by CPI UK

Pen & Sword Books Limited incorporates the imprints of Atlas, Archaeology, Aviation, Discovery, Family History, Fiction, History, Maritime, Military, Military Classics, Politics, Select, Transport, True Crime, Air World, Frontline Publishing, Leo Cooper, Remember When, Seaforth Publishing, The Praetorian Press, Wharncliffe Local History, Wharncliffe Transport, Wharncliffe True Crime and White Owl.

For a complete list of Pen & Sword titles please contact

PEN & SWORD BOOKS LIMITED
47 Church Street, Barnsley, South Yorkshire, S70 2AS, England
E-mail: enquiries@pen-and-sword.co.uk
Website: www.pen-and-sword.co.uk

Or
PEN AND SWORD BOOKS
1950 Lawrence Rd, Havertown, PA 19083, USA
E-mail: Uspen-and-sword@casematepublishers.com
Website: www.penandswordbooks.com

Contents

An early morning sunrise over RAF Muharraq (Bahrain) in 1963 catches 8 Squadron FGA.9s being readied for an exercise. (Ray Deacon)

Acknowledgements

I am most grateful to all the photographers credited in this book. There are too many to name but I am especially indebted to Ray Deacon (and friends) and Simon Watson at the Aviation Bookshop who very kindly allowed me to use some rare photos. Among the many Websites that stand out include the one on Omani Hunters posted by I. Hawkridge, which apart from images contains much information on the aircraft. Finally, I must pay homage to the late Francis K. Mason, a former Hawker man and superb author, whose listing by serial number of every Hunter built in *Hawker Hunter: Biography of a thoroughbred* published in 1985 is as indispensible today as it was then.

Martin W. Bowman, Norwich, 2020

Introduction

If ever there was a real pilot's aeroplane it was the Hunter, an outstanding multi-purpose aircraft which excelled in the roles of interceptor fighter, ground attack, reconnaissance, research vehicle and two-seater trainer and not forgetting the dramatic formation aerobatic performances.

British fighters had been among the World's finest during World War Two. Many of them, such as the Hawker Hurricane and the Typhoon rocket-firing fighter, were the result of the design teams headed by Sydney Camm, a man who had been Hawker's Chief Designer since 1925. His greatest post-war creation, the Hunter, beckoned, but bringing this project (and others) to fruition would prove difficult. Work on the Hunter commenced late in 1948, but because of the depressed post-war economic situation in Britain it was not until early 1950 that Hunter prototypes were constructed. Neville Duke made the first flight on 20 July 1951 and on 19 September 1953 he piloted a Hunter to shatter the world air speed record.

The Hunter is one of the World's greatest aircraft which for three decades pilots enthused about, extolling the smooth aerodynamic lines, four 30mm cannon, the Rolls-Royce Avon engine, outstandingly honest handling characteristics combined with a lively performance. Who can ever forget the glory days of the unforgettable aerobatic displays with the 'Black Knights', 'Black Arrows' and 'Blue Diamonds'. It vividly recalls operations in Europe with Fighter Command and 2nd TAF and in Cyprus, the Middle East and the Far East, where Hunters in the ground attack role operated against rebels in Aden and Malaysia respectively. The Hunter also saw combat service in a range of conflicts with several operators, including the Suez Crisis, the Sino-Indian War, the Indo-Pakistani War of 1965, the Indo-Pakistani War of 1971, the Rhodesian Bush War, the Second Congo War, the Six-Day War, the War of Attrition, the Yom Kippur War and the 2007 Lebanon conflict.

Apart from Britain, where Hunter aircraft flew in forty RAF and five Royal Navy squadrons, Hunters served in nineteen overseas air forces including, India, Jordan, Iraq, Switzerland and Chile. Of the 1,972 Hunters manufactured in the UK and under licence in Holland and Belgium, 526 aircraft were returned to Hawker Siddeley Aircraft and rebuilt to as new condition to fulfil new orders and no fewer than 21 countries purchased new and refurbished examples during 1954-1975.

This incredible achievement is often overlooked in comparison to the Lockheed Starfighter which was produced by manufacturers in seven countries including a multinational programme in Europe that turned out 996 Starfighters and went on to equip fifteen air forces. Starfighter production however, eventually reached 2,559.

Plans to produce a supersonic Hunter (P.1083), using an afterburning R.A.14 Avon engine and 50° swept wing, ended on 13 July 1953 with the cancellation of the prototype. If the change in wing sweep had gone ahead, the P.1083 might well have achieved supersonic performance in level flight.

The Hunter was undoubtedly a classic thoroughbred of its time form the stables of one of the finest fighter manufacturers in the world. The Hunter's success assured for fifty years its longevity and adaptability was rarely challenged, the last example being retired in July 2001. The Hunter legend lives on, however, with over a hundred potentially airworthy airframes located in fourteen countries around the world.

Work in progress on the first prototype P. 1067 WB188 approaching completion in experimental works at Richmond Road. (BAe)

Above: During 1955-56 Fokker-Aviolanda in Amsterdam produced 96 F.4s and 93 F.6s for the Koninklijke Luchtmacht (Royal Netherlands Air Force) and some of the Belgian machines. In Holland these served in the Koninklijke Luchtmacht on 323, 324 and 325 Squadrons at Leeuwarden and 326 and 327 Squadrons at Soesterberg. The F.4s operated between 1955-1964, while the F.6 operated between 1957 and 1968.

Opposite: HSA advertisement announcing the acquisition by Peru of the Hawker Hunter for its air force.

Hunters Defend PERU

Speed, offensive power and great versatility have given the Hawker Hunter pride of place in the air forces of many countries, including Peru. Today several squadrons of Hunters are in service with the Peruvian air force, forging another sturdy link in the defences of the free world. Hunters are also in service in India, Denmark, Holland, Belgium, Sweden, Iraq — and now Switzerland.

HAWKER AIRCRAFT LIMITED Kingston-on-Thames, England
MEMBER OF HAWKER SIDDELEY / ONE OF THE WORLD'S INDUSTRIAL LEADERS

CHAPTER 1

A Hunter We Will Go

In Britain in November 1946 the specification for the first swept wing jet powered by the 5,000lb thrust Nene 2 was issued. Eight months earlier, three prototypes of Hawker Aircraft's first jet fighter, the P.1040, which was adapted for carrier-based interception, had been ordered. The first P.1040 prototype flew on 2 September 1947 powered by a 4,500lb thrust Rolls-Royce Nene I, which produced a maximum speed of about Mach 0.77 (510 mph). An increase in speed and performance only resulted when Camm forged ahead with plans for a swept-wing design, designated the P.1047, powered by a more powerful Nene engine. The new wings had a sweepback of 35 degrees on the quarter chord and a thickness ratio of 0.10. By the end of 1947 Sydney Camm and his design team at Richmond Road, Kingston-upon-Thames knew they would have to design an aircraft that could accommodate the new 6,500 lb Rolls-Royce A.J.65 axial-flow turbojet. This engine would soon become world famous as the Avon. Specification F.3/48 was issued to Hawkers early in 1948 for a single-seat, cannon armed, day interceptor fighter capable of Mach 0.94 (620 mph at 36,000 feet, 724 mph at sea level) and have an endurance of sixty minutes. An ejection seat would be mandatory and provision had to be made for a future radar-ranging gunsight. The main characteristics of Camm's original P.1067 design included an Avon engine mounted in the fuselage amidships with annular nose air intake and exhausting through a long jet pipe in the extreme tail. The wing was swept back 42½ degrees on the quarter-chord and a straight-tapered tailplane was mounted on top of the fin, though this was later deleted.

The P.1067 was the only single-seat, single-engined fighter in the world designed to carry four cannon. But indecision surrounded the choice of gun and the engine to power the P.1067. In 1949 finally, four 30mm Aden cannon armament fit was adopted, cleverly mounted with their magazines in a removable gun-pack located behind the cockpit but problems occurred because ejected cannon ammunition links had a tendency to strike and damage the underside of the fuselage and diverting the gas emitted by the cannon during firing was another necessary modification. The original split-flap airbrakes caused adverse changes in pitch trim and were quickly replaced by a single ventral airbrake. This meant, however, that the airbrake could not be used for landings. WB188, the first of the three prototypes and WB195 were powered by the Avon, while the Armstrong-Siddeley Sapphire powered WB202. This aircraft went on to become the prototype F.2. Being powered by the Armstrong-Siddeley Sapphire engine, the F.2 did not suffer from the occurrence of surging and stalling with the Avon engines. Hawkers would build 139 Avon-powered F.1s and Armstrong-Whitworth 45 Sapphire-engined Mk.2s before production switched to the F.4.

Work on the three prototypes continued throughout 1950-51. WB188 was painted a glossy pale duck egg green finish and on 1 July 1951 Chief Test Pilot. Squadron Leader Neville Duke carried out WB188's first engine run. On 20 July he flew the prototype on a 47-minute flight and two months later Duke was making high-speed passes in excess of 700 mph at the Farnborough Air Show.

On 5 May 1952 Duke flew WB195, the second P.1067, now officially called 'Hunter' from the new Hawker test field at Dunsfold, Surrey. WB195 differed from WB188 in having a production R.A. (Reheated Avon) 7 and full military equipment, including four Aden cannon and radar ranging gunsight. On 4 June Neville Duke put WB195 through its paces at West Raynham in front of the RAF's Central Fighter Establishment, which would be the first to receive production Hunters prior to their entry into squadron service. On 10 July 1952 Duke flew WB188 at the Brussels Air Show in front of a large and very appreciative crowd. The Hunter's triumphant public debut was at that year's September SBAC show at Farnborough where WB195 was flown each day with WB188 held in reserve. The occasion was overshadowed by the loss on 6 September of the de Havilland DH.110 prototype, its pilot, John Derry and his fellow crewmember Anthony Richards. Thirty people on the ground were killed and 63 people were injured. In spite of the tragedy Neville Duke followed with a truly brilliant flying display, which included a transonic dive. Duke flew WB202, the third P.1067 prototype, for the first time on 30 November 1952.

It was evident that having just the three prototypes was woefully inadequate and the first twenty production F.1s came to be regarded as development machines, being used to test numerous trial installations including an area-ruled fuselage, blown flaps and alternative styles of air brake. Limited fuel capacity reduced the F.1 endurance substantially and there was the problem of rapid pitch up, which began to occur in some manoeuvres at the higher subsonic Mach numbers without adequate warning. There were severe compressor surge problems with the Avon 104 and to a lesser extent, the Mk.113 engine. Engine surging noticeably increased when gun gases were ingested during high altitude gun firing. Diving to increase airspeed and to reduce altitude usually effected recovery from the surge but engine flame out often resulted. These problems were finally eliminated with the introduction of the surge-free R.A.21. The 8,000 lb thrust Sapphire 101 engined F.2 had no such engine surge problems and gun firing was cleared up to 47,000 feet. Also, the Sapphire could develop slightly more thrust at lower specific fuel consumption than the Avon as fitted to the F.1. Even so, except for 105 Sapphire-powered F.5s, Avon engines powered all the Hunters in service. Frank Murphy flew WT555, the first production F.1, at Dunsfold on 16 May 1953 but the F.1 would not finally enter service until late in July 1954.

In 1953 WB188 was modified for an attempt to break the World Absolute Air Speed Record, which stood at 715.75 mph set by an F-86D Sabre. In August WB188 was adapted to take an R.A.7R Avon capable of 7,130 lb thrust 'dry' and 9,600 lb with reheat lit. The Hunter, which was painted bright red overall and designated the Mk.3, also received a sharply pointed nose cone fairing and a windscreen fairing. Operating from Tangmere, Sussex on 7 September, Neville Duke made practice runs in WB188 along the 3km course off the coast of Rustington, achieving an average speed of 727.63 mph (Mach 0.92 at sea level). On 19 September Duke flew WB188 round a 100-kilometre closed circuit to set a new world record for this course at 709.2 mph. Shortly afterwards the Supermarine Swift broke Duke's record flying at 735.70 mph in Libya where higher ambient temperatures greatly assisted the record breaking attempt.

The first of 365 F.4s flew on 20 October 1954. All were built with a 'full flying tail' and they were powered by the Avon R.A.7 rated 113 or 115; the latter modified to reduce engine surge. Fuel capacity was increased by the installation of bigger internal fuel cells and two 100-gallon drop tanks on inboard wing pylons. Provision was made for underwing stores. The first of 105 Sapphire powered Armstrong-Whitworth built F.5s flew on 19 October 1954. The Hunter F.4 had only a short career with the majority of squadrons in Germany. After the scrapping of numerous F.4 and F.5 airframes during 1960-63 it became cost-effective to re-build F.4s to take the bigger, more powerful Avon 200-series engine. The P.1101 trainer prototype (XJ615) flew for the first time on 8 July 1955. The two seater was powered by the same Avon 113 as fitted to the F.4, but the second prototype (XJ627), which was based on the F.6 and which flew on 17 November 1956, was powered by the more powerful Avon 203, which produced 10,000 lb of thrust and was fitted to XF833, which became the first F.6. This engine was not adopted on production aircraft however. The first T.7, production model (XL563) flew on 11 October 1957. The 45 T.7s built differed from the fighter versions in having a nose lengthened by 3 feet. At first the T.7 was armed with two cannon in the nose but this was later reduced to just one gun with the deletion of the port Aden. During 1957-58 six more T.7s were converted from F.4 airframes and these were delivered between February and May 1959.

The F.6 was really a new aircraft designed as an interceptor but developed with the ground attack role in mind. It evolved from the P.1099, which was created by marrying uprated production wings to the redundant P.1083 fuselage and installing the Rolls-Royce Avon R.A.14 engine, which by April 1952 was producing 10,500 lbs static thrust. Some other revisions on the F.6 included a revised fuel tank layout, the centre fuselage tanks being replaced by new ones in the rear fuselage; the 'Mod 228' wing, which has a distinctive 'dogtooth' leading edge notch to alleviate the pitch-up problem; and four 'wet' hardpoints, finally giving the aircraft a good ferry range. Experienced Hunter pilots noticed the difference immediately. In addition to inboard 1,000 lb bombs or 100-gallon drop tanks four rocket tiers were mounted under each outer wing so that up to 24 3-inch rocket projectiles could be carried. Neville Duke flew the P.1099 prototype (XF833) on 23 January 1954. The new engine was then derated to 10,000 lbs static thrust and became the Avon 203. On 20 July 1954 P.1099 flight trials were resumed and were successful. Seven F.1 airframes were quickly converted to 'interim Mk.6' standard to serve as pre-production aircraft. Bill Bedford flew WW592, the first, on 25 March 1955. By mid-1956 just over 100 F.6s had been built. Early production models were fitted with a variable-incidence tailplane, just as on previous marks, but all subsequent F.6 models had a 'flying tail' and extended-chord dog-tooth wing.

A conversion contract to modify 33 F.6 aircraft to FR.10 standard for the reconnaissance role was received in 1958 to meet a need to replace the Supermarine Swift FR.5 in 2nd Tactical Air Force (2nd TAF) in Germany and the Meteor FR.9 in the Far East. The FR.10 differed principally from the F.6 in having three forward-looking reconnaissance cameras in the nose where they replaced the radar ranging scanner and camera gun. The four Aden cannon were retained for a secondary air defence role if required. Armour plate had to be fitted under the cockpit floor as ballast. The FR.10 had the same tail parachute and 230 gallon drop tank capability of the FGA.9, which gave a LO-LO radius of 240nm and a HI-LO-HI radius of 570nm which meant that the FR.10 could fly from Germany to Malta non-stop if required. XF429, the first conversion, flew for the first time on 7 November 1958. Starting in September 1960 Nos. 2 and 4 Squadrons at Gütersloh received FR.10s to form RAF Germany's Tactical Reconnaissance Wing. Four or five FR.10s were also assigned to 1417 Flight at Khormaksar in Aden. Several other Hunter squadrons were issued with one or two FR 10s to provide them with a photo-reconnaissance capability. The aircraft remained in RAF service until 1971/72 when they began to be replaced by the F-4 Phantom. The RN also operated four PR.11s (Mk.11 Hunters equipped with the FR.10 camera nose) and these were flown by FRADU to help work-up ships' crews before operational deployments.

In May 1958 the first of 41 T.8, -B and -C dual-control trainers for the Royal Navy's swept-wing carrier aircraft programme were delivered to 764 Training Squadron at RNAS Lossiemouth. F.4 WW664, which was converted to two-seat configuration, effectively became the prototype T.8 and 27 first phase T.8s followed. During 1958-59 eighteen F.4s were brought up to T.8 standard. In 1963 a Navy requirement for operational training on the Tactical Air Navigation (TACAN) system led to the delivery of four T.8B aircraft with full TACAN equipment. An order for ten F.4s to be converted to T.8C with partial TACAN equipment followed.

In July 1954 about twelve newly modified F.1s were issued to the CFE at West Raynham and 43 Squadron at RAF Leuchars, Scotland began receiving its first F.1s, becoming fully operational by October. Late in 1954-early 1955 four more first-line squadrons received F.1s and F.2s. The engine surge problems associated with the F.1 restricted all other deliveries to Operational Conversion Units (OCUs). The Empire Test Pilots School at RAE Farnborough and the Fighter Weapons School at Leconfield, Yorkshire, also operated F.1s and F.2s. In April 1955 F.4s began arriving at West Raynham for use with the Air Fighting Development Squadron (AFDS) and DFLS. During the year F.4s re-equipped three front line squadrons and 229 OCU at Chivenor and the Flying College at Manby, Lincolnshire also took delivery of the F.4.

The first F.5 made its maiden flight on 19 October 1954, the day before the first Mk.4 and a total of 105 was built by August 1955. The F.5 entered service with six home-based squadrons, all during 1955. No.263 Squadron was the first to receive the new aircraft, replacing its F.2s from March that year. Between May and July Nos. 56, 41, 1 and 257 Squadrons received the F.5, replacing the Supermarine Swift, Meteor F.8 (41 and 1) and the Hunter F.2. Finally in December, 34 Squadron began to convert to the F.5. Replacement of five squadrons of Armstrong Siddeley Sapphire-engined F.2s, Meteor F.8s and Swifts with F.5s occurred in 1955. The Sapphire had the same improvements as on the Rolls-Royce powered Mk.4, with an increase in the internal fuel supply and the addition of underwing pylons that could carry 100 gallon drop tanks or 1,000 lbs of bombs each. One of the F.5s was used to test the 10,000 lb Sapphire ASSa.7 engine, in case of problems with the Rolls-Royce Avon 203 engine that was to be used in the F.Mk.6. At this stage the Sapphire 7 disappointed, suffering from lubrication problems that slowly reduced its rated power. The climb rate was also not as good as expected and after the problems with the large Avon engine were solved, no more work was conducted on new Sapphire powered Hunters. Instead Armstrong Whitworth converted to production of the F.6. In 1956 seven fighter squadrons were equipped with the F.4 in the UK and thirteen in 2nd Tactical Air Force, where it replaced all ten squadrons of Sabre F.1/F.4s in the Brüggen, Geilenkirchen, Jever, Oldenburg and Wildenrath wings and the three DH Venom FB.1 Squadrons of the Fassberg Wing. The Jever Wing became the first in Germany to receive the F.4, eventually becoming a four squadron Hunter wing operating in the dual role of air defence and ground attack.

The F.5 was the first RAF version of the Hunter to see active service when in October Nos. 1 and 34 Squadrons flew them to Nicosia in Cyprus to be in position to support British and French aircraft involved in Operation 'Musketeer', the Anglo-French occupation of the Suez Canal zone. The F.5's greater fuel capacity allowed them to operate over Egypt and at first they were used to provide top cover for RAF Canberra and Valiant bombers and Royal Navy carrier aircraft carrying out attacks on Egyptian airfields. Their limited endurance permitted only a short time over the patrol area but it soon became clear that no air-to-air combat was going to take place and on 2 November the Hunters carrying the yellow and black Suez identification stripes were used as base defence aircraft at Akrotiri and Nicosia to protect against possible hit-and-run attacks by Egyptian Il-28s. No such raids took place although two were destroyed on the ground by terrorists and the two F.5 squadrons returned home without having fired their guns in anger. During 1958 heightened tension in Cyprus, Jordan and the Lebanon saw Hunters being based in Nicosia and these were often supported by detachments from the UK. The F.5 had a short front-line career - 1 Squadron was the last squadron to use it, disbanding as a Hunter squadron on 23 June 1958.

Meanwhile, at home the first F.6s had, in 1956, begun re-equipping four squadrons and seven more followed suit in 1957 when, ironically, Duncan Sandys' infamous Defence White Paper predicted that the ICBM would shortly render manned interceptor aircraft obsolete. HM Government reduced the number of F.6s for the RAF by 100 aircraft and a 1955 order for fifty F.6s was cancelled. Nine of the thirteen F.4 squadrons in 2nd TAF were disbanded almost immediately. At Hawkers the crisis of confidence caused by Sandys' White Paper was largely overcome with the introduction of the ground attack Hunter and F.4 production being further increased in the late 1950s-early 1960s to meet the needs of several overseas air forces. By the end of 1958 all Hunter squadrons in Fighter Command and the five F.4 Squadrons in Germany had completed re-equipment with Hunter F.6s. That same year, T.7s entered RAF service on 229 OCU at Chivenor. Later examples were issued to operational squadrons in Fighter Command and 2nd TAF in Germany.

Squadron Leader Neville Duke with the P.1067 Hunter prototype WB188 in at Dunsfold in 1951. The P.1067 first flew from RAF Boscombe Down on 20 July 1951 powered by a 6,500 lb Avon 103 engine. The second prototype, which was fitted with production avionics, armament and a 7,550 lb Avon 107 turbojet, first flew on 5 May 1952. As an insurance against Avon development problems, Hawker modified the design to accommodate another axial turbojet, the 8,000 lb Armstrong Siddeley Sapphire 101. Fitted with a Sapphire, the third prototype flew on 30 November 1952. (BAe)

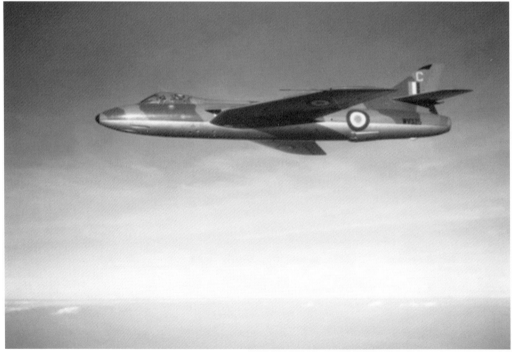

Above: The purpose of the annual air defence exercise 25-27 May 1957, Exercise 'Vigilant' was to ensure that in the event of an atomic attack against Great Britain, Fighter Command, in the words of the AOC-in-C, Air Marshal Sir Thomas Pike, would be 'on the ball the very first day.' And so, to give the Command practice in resisting the first atomic raid of any future war, 'Vigilant' consisted of a simulation of that first raid and was repeated a further eight times during the three-day exercise. The Hunters on 74 'Tiger' Squadron at Horsham St. Faith (now Norwich Airport) achieved a high interception rate during the exercise and they were particularly pleased with a turnaround time of twelve minutes for each aircraft under the stringent conditions imposed. Normal practice was for two aircraft to be constantly on standby to scramble or to replace those aircraft already in the air and whose fuel was getting low. Based squadrons would take turns at filling this very short notice alert. An interesting feature of the night activity was the presence of three squadrons of Javelins - 46 Squadron Mk.1s from Odiham and (pictured in the background) Coltishall squadrons Nos. 141 and 23, both recently re-equipped with the Mk.4 Javelins - operating from Horsham St. Faith because the runway at Coltishall was being re-surfaced.

Opposite above: F.6 XF523 which was issued to 54 Squadron before being converted to FGA.Mk.9. It crashed and was SOC on 24 June 1963.

Opposite below: To address the problem of range, a production F.1 was fitted with a modified wing featuring bag-type fuel tanks in the leading edge and 'wet' hardpoints. The resulting F.4 first flew on 20 October 1954 and entered service in March 1955. A distinctive feature added on the F.4 was the pair of blisters under the cockpit, which collected spent ammunition links to prevent airframe damage. Crews dubbed these 'Sabrinas' after the contemporary buxom film star. The Sapphire-powered version of the F.4 was designated the F.5. F. Mk.4 WV325 (pictured in almost certainly late summer 1955 when it was on the CFS), which first flew on 13 June 1955, returned to HAL on 19 October 1967 for conversion to Jordanian FGA.Mk.73A (846) and was delivered to Jordan on 7 October 1971. (Mike Stroud)

F.Mk.5 WP183/V on 56 Squadron in flight from RAF Waterbeach having been delivered to the Squadron in June 1955. In 1952 and 1953 56 Squadron flew the Meteor F.8 at Waterbeach receiving the Swift for evaluation in 1953 until 1955. In September 1957 the squadron moved to RAF Wattisham with the F.5/F.6 where they would spend 35 years defending UK airspace. The F.5 saw action during Operation 'Musketeer', the Anglo-French-Israeli seizure of the Suez Canal in late 1956. Hunters flew from Cyprus to provide top cover for air strikes on Egyptian airfields and to provide air defence against Egyptian bombers.

Above: F.6 XK138/M which first flew on 21 May 1957, being delivered to 5 MU on 27 May that same year, before being issued to 14 Squadron and was coded 'Y'. It went onto serve on 20 Squadron.

Opposite: F.Mk.1s WT594/U, WT622/G and WT641/T on 43 Squadron during one of their impressive aerobatic routines. It was at Leuchars in July 1954 that the Squadron became the first in the RAF to be equipped with Hunters. By 1955 the Squadron had become the official aerobatic team, giving displays not only in Britain but all over Europe. During this period the 'Fighting Cocks' beat eight other nations including the French and American Air Forces to win the only ever international formation aerobatics competition in Rome. In April 1956 the Squadron had the honour to perform before and considerably impress Nikolai Bulganin and Nikita Khrushchev of the Soviet Union during their visit to Britain.

F.4 WV406/F on 222 Squadron at Leuchars, Scotland with the Officers Mess in the background in the summer of 1957. This Hunter first flew on 9 September 1955 and served later on 229 OCU at Chivenor and No.3 CAACU (Combined Anti-Aircraft Co-Operation Unit) at Exeter. (Croup Captain Ed Durham)

T.7 XL583/'ES-84' on 229 OCU at Chivenor in December 1958. This two-seater was delivered to the OCU on 1 July 1958 and later saw service at RNAS Brawdy, from November 1976 and the TWU from 1978 before joining No.2 TWU (as '84') in 1981. XL583 crashed during landing approach at Brawdy on 1 December 1981 after the failure of a diaphragm in the engine control system. Flight Lieutenant R. E. Lotinga and Flight Lieutenant D. K. Wakefield ejected while on approach to Brawdy, the aircraft coming down one-and-a-half miles north of Brawdy. Both pilots were injured.

CHAPTER 2

The Hunter's Halcyon Days

In the 1950s and early 1960s the RAF team selected to give aerobatic displays did so while retaining a first-line operational capability. In 1956 'Treble One' Squadron, which was equipped with F.4s and commanded by Squadron Leader Roger L. Topp AFC* provided RAF Fighter Command's aerobatic reserve team. For the first time since the war, the RAF permitted an aerobatic team to paint its aircraft in a special display finish and black was finally chosen. In 1956 a leading French newspaper had dubbed the team *les Fleches Volantes* ('Flying Arrows'). In June 1957 at the 22nd Paris Salon display, the team, which was only one in Europe regularly flying five swept-wing aircraft, was described as *les Fleches Noir* and the 'Black Arrows' was born. By the summer of 1958 jet-pipe smoke generators were fitted to the F.6s and thus the team was able to produce bold smoke trails to trace the pattern of its manoeuvres. That year the team flew most of their 24 major displays in seven countries with five Hunters but there were rumours of a larger number of aircraft being flown by other air forces. The 'Black Arrows' thought of a sixteen formation, the squadron's full complement of aircraft. Then it was felt that they could make a really big impact at Farnborough in September with something even larger. 'Boss' Topp considered many weird and wonderful shapes and eventually came up with 21 aircraft in seven echelons of three. But he felt that that there was something missing, so he added one more. They would go for a 22 Hunter loop!

Twenty-six serviceable Hunters were required so extra pilots and Hunters had to be borrowed from other squadrons. Not every squadron wanted to give up their 'aces' or their best Hunters but eventually, the numbers were achieved. The 22-loop conceived by Roger Topp was purely a build up from doing something more than the sixteen and it more or less evolved as they tried to get something that made sense to look at, had impact and was feasible to fly. Twenty-two aircraft provided a spare aircraft within the formation. Once committed to the run in there was no way spares could be used so if there was a failure everyone would move up their own line and the 22nd aircraft could fill in the gap. At Odiham on 1 September the team practiced in the morning and gave their first display that afternoon in front of 7,300 VIPs and guests in the trade stands at Farnborough.

In October 1958 Roger Topp, who had formed and developed the team, which had gained a worldwide reputation for the skill and precision of its formation aerobatics over three years, was posted and Squadron Leader Peter A. Latham AFC had the distinction of taking over the squadron at Wattisham. In 1960 'Treble One' once again provided the leading aerobatic team of Fighter Command. In 1961 and 1962, 92 Squadron's 'Blue Diamonds' aerobatic team carried on the proud Hunter tradition set by 'Treble One' with the F.6. 'Shiny Blue' was commanded by Squadron Leader Brian Mercer AFC. Often the 'Blue Diamonds' flew three practice shows a day, in addition to their operational flying. The normal repertoire with nine aircraft saw each event being separated by a wing-over or a tight turn in front of the crowd: - Diamond Nine loop; Diamond Nine roll, with smoke; T-bone loop, with smoke; Delta roll; Wine-glass loop (breaking 4 and 5); Half-Swan roll, with smoke; Line-abreast loop (breaking 6 and 7); Box-Five roll, with smoke; Bomb-burst loop, with smoke. After the Hunters had re-formed into two echelons they came in and executed a double loop in echelon. The basic box-four formation readily lends itself to expansion and while initially the team consisted of nine aircraft it could easily be increased to 12 or 16 aircraft, allowing in the sixteen-aircraft team four split formations of four aircraft each. 1962 was The 'Blue Diamonds' last season as a Hunter display team. For the 1963 season the 'Firebirds' of 56 (Lightning) Squadron was selected as the official RAF aerobatic team. Two years later the 'Red Arrows' performed in public for the first time and in 1969 the 'Reds' were established on a permanent basis within the CFS as a squadron in their own right.

Opposite above: 'Black Arrows' F.6 XG194/X was first flown on 6 September 1956 and delivered to 43 Squadron and later issued to 111 Squadron at RAF Wattisham where it was flown by the CO, Squadron Leader Roger Topp. Later, it flew on 92 Squadron before being converted to FGA. Mk.9 in March 1965 and then served on 1 Squadron and RNAS Brawdy. When the aircraft was finally grounded it was modified to resemble a Soviet MiG and put on the edge of the RAF North Luffenham runway (now St. George's Barracks) as a Cold War target. Now fully restored, Wattisham Airfield Museum has named the Hunter 'Blackjack Red One' in 'Boss' Topp's honour.

Opposite below: Five 'Black Arrows' in line abreast formation.

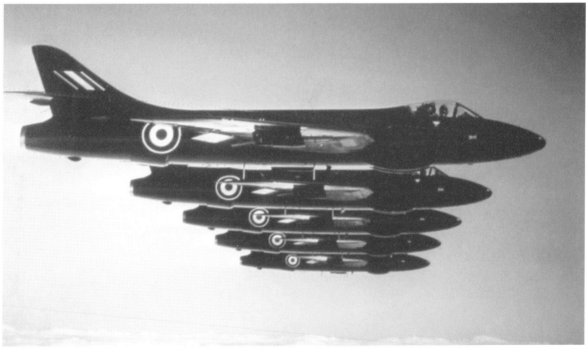

16

Above: 'Black Arrows' in a sixteen ship formation at Farnborough in 1960.

Opposite above: A section of Treble One's T.7 WV318 and two F.6s taking off from Farnborough on 13 September 1959. Originally built as an F.4, WV318 is one of only three F.4s with wing leading-edge extensions. The aircraft flew for the first time on 23 May 1955 and was delivered to 5MU at RAF Kemble on 16 June, serving on Nos.14 and 93 Squadrons before an accident in March 1956 saw WV318 returned to Hawkers for repairs. While there conversion to T.7 took place and reissue to the RAF occurred on 1 June 1959. It saw service on 111 Squadron and the Central Flying School before being converted to T.7A in 1964. Used as a trainer and hack by 74 and 5 Squadrons flying the Lightning. In February 1970 WV318 was issued to 12 Squadron, which was equipped with the Buccaneer and went on to perform similar duties on 15 and 16 Squadrons RAFG, the Laarbruch Station Flight and 237 OCU from 1980, before ending up at Lossiemouth on 208 Squadron. When the aircraft was retired it was painted black along with the other three Hunters at Lossiemouth to commemorate 40 years of the type and carried the 111 Squadron crest. Purchased in early 1996 by Delta Jets it was flown to Kemble and then underwent a complete overhaul back to airworthiness, returning to the air on 2 May 1996. WV318 is now based at Cranfield and makes regular air show appearances.

Opposite below: The 'Black Arrows' in formation on 18 June 1959 photographed by *Stars and Stripes*' 'Red' Grandy from the T.7 flown by Flight Lieutenant Patrick B. Hine during a practice flight. Air Chief Marshal Sir Patrick 'Paddy' Bardon Hine GCB GBE served as joint commander of British forces during the Gulf War.

A 'Treble One' Squadron pilot in the cockpit of F.6 XG171 at RAF Wattisham. This Hunter first flew on 23 August 1956 and was delivered on 24 September that same year. It was issued to 43 Squadron and then it joined 111 Squadron before being sold to the Royal Jordanian Air Force in 1962.

A vast array of weapons available for the FGA.9 at Farnborough in 1959 in front of XG135. (Ian Cadwallader)

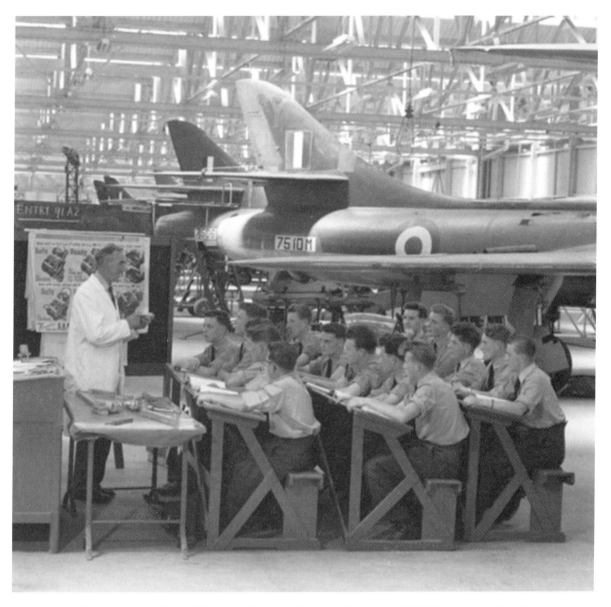

Aircraft apprentices of Entry 91 at No. 1 School of Technical Training at RAF Halton Apprentices School near Wendover in Buckinghamshire receiving 'Final Airframes' training from Mr. Maynall in a classroom hangar containing F.1 instructional airframes in July 1959. In 1919 Lord Trenchard established the No. 1 School of Technical Training at RAF Halton for RAF aircraft apprentices, which remained at the station until it moved to RAF Cosford in 1993.

Above: F.4 WW663 on 14 Squadron was delivered to the RAF on 27 April 1955. Shortly after re-equipment with the F.4 that year, 14 Squadron was transferred from Fassberg to Oldenburg where it joined 124 Wing in the day fighter role. The contraction of the RAF after the 1957 Defence White Paper caused subsequent moves to Alhorn in 1957 and then to Gütersloh in 1958. While at Alhorn the Squadron received the F.6, which it operated until, as the last Day Fighter squadron in RAF Germany, it disbanded on 17 December 1962. WW663 was broken up at Chilbolton that same year.

Opposite above: 'Formation Friday' - 79 Squadron Swift FR.5s on 79 Squadron and Hunter F.6s on 14 and 20 Squadrons of the Gütersloh Wing in June 1960. The Swift FR.5s on 79 Squadron were replaced by Hunter FR.10s in January 1961.

Opposite below: Hunter F.6 in the colours of XG152 on IV Squadron RAF Germany on display at the Luftwaffe Museum at Berlin-Gatow. The squadron badge is a sun in splendour divided per bend by a flash of lightning - approved by HRH King Edward VIII in May 1936. The red and black segmented sun suggests round-the-clock operations, while the lightning flash is a reference to the unit's early use of wireless telephony for artillery co-operation.

Above: Hunter F.4 XF986/A, which was delivered to 33 MU on 12 June 1956 and issued to 112 Squadron at Brüggen. It later operated on 234 Squadron and was then issued to 229 OCU. On 7 August 1959 it was being flown by Flying Officer A. J. B. Bametson who failed to recover from a spin during aerobatics and it hit the ground at Youlton Farm, Sutcome, Southwest of Bideford, Devon after he had ejected over Milton Dameral.

Opposite above: An early 'load combination' image illustrating the Hunter's ability to carry 230-gallon, 100-gallon drop tanks, 1,000 lb and 500 lb bombs, practice bombs, HVAR, three-inch and two-inch rockets, Fireflash and Firestreak air-to-air missiles in addition to its four 30 mm Aden cannon.

Opposite below: The distinctive tiger markings of F.6 XF511 of 74 Squadron at Horsham St. Faith in 1960. XF511 later operated on 111 Squadron and was converted to FGA.Mk.9 before joining 8 Squadron and subsequently RNAS Brawdy, in October 1976 and the TWU, from 1978. 74 Squadron operated Hunters from 1957 to 1960. (Ray Deacon collection)

Above: F.6 XG164/H on 74 'Tiger' Squadron in flight. This Hunter also served on 33 MU, 111 Squadron and the West Raynham Station Flight before being transferred to the FAA at RNAS Brawdy in October 1976. It last served on the TWU (Tactical Weapons Unit) in 1978.

Opposite: The 'Blue Diamonds' diving down for a bomb burst over Cyprus in 1961. 'G' is XG232 which first flew on 13 October 1956. It was first issued to 92 Squadron and later served on the A&AEE before being purchased by Hawker Siddeley Aircraft on 21 June 1966 for conversion to Chilean FGA. Mk.71 (J-714) for delivery on 19 June 1968. (Brian Allchin)

Above: The 'Blue Diamonds' in line abreast formation. (Brian Allchin)

Opposite: The 'Blue Diamonds' climbing in tight formation over Cyprus in 1961. (Brian Allchin)

Above: The 'Blue Diamonds' photographed looping over Cyprus in early 1961 by Flying Officer Brian Allchin from the right-hand seat of T.7 XL605/T piloted by the OC, Squadron Leader Brian Mercer. The two-seater and XF451 (borrowed from 229 OCU) had not yet been painted in blue livery. XF451 was SOC after a landing accident on 20 July 1962. XL605, which first flew on 14 October 1958 was purchased by HSA on 6 April 1966 and converted to Saudi Arabian T.Mk.70 (70-617), being delivered to that country on 7 June. It returned to the RAF in July 1974 and was issued to 229 OCU as XX467. In 1997 it was slowly rebuilt with components from XF358 and registered as G-TVII. It is now displayed at the Newark Air Museum. (Brian Allchin)

Opposite above: The 'Blue Diamonds' at Meherab, Iran on 20 October 1961 with Armée de l' Air (French Air Force) Dassault Mystère IVAs. That month 92 Squadron performed displays at Akrotiri, Nicosia and Episkopi in Cyprus, on 14, 16 and 17 October respectively, as well as one in front of the Crown Prince of Greece at Elefsis, on 23 October. This Hunter first flew on 29 March 1958 and was used on 229 OCU before it was issued to 92 Squadron. It finished its service on the TWU in 1976-77. In June 1962 when the RAF won the NATO AIRCENT gun firing competition for the first time 'Shiny Blue' used F.6s and their 30mm cannon to eclipse RCAF Sabres, which traditionally used .5 inch machine guns to win this completion in the past. The .5 inch machine gun was much easier to harmonize and the Sabre was a very stable gun platform. The Hunter was a 'livelier' aircraft and the 30mm cannon was 'quite a handful'. (Brian Allchin)

Opposite below: An instructor shows Aircraft Apprentices of No.1 School of Technical Training at RAF Halton how to load an Aden gun pack of four 30mm cannon into an instructional airframe in 1961.

F.5 WN990 which was delivered to 45 MU on 6 April 1955 and was issued to 263 Squadron before going to 56 Squadron and then the RAF Wattisham Station Flight. It was purchased by HSA and scrapped in 1962. (Noel Collier, Air Britain Coll)

CHAPTER 3

Detached Service

Early in 1960 a detachment to RRAF Thornhill in Rhodesia was made by Hunters from Khormaksar in Aden. The pilot of FGA.9 XG136/C listens for the AVPIN to ignite as Herbie Nute casually leans on the drop tank. The automatic starting cycle on the Avon-200 series Hunters was initiated by an AVPIN (isopropyl nitrate liquid fuel starter) which fired for around seven seconds. The system was usually reliable but on occasions an engine would fail to light-up, leaving a pool of fuel in the jet pipe. After a short wait, the sequence known as a 'wet start' was tried again and flames would extend from the jet pipe. (Bill Horspole)

FGA.9s on 208 Squadron (left), 54 and XG207/F on 1 Squadron (right) at Kuwait New Airport during the first Gulf Crisis of July 1961. (As part of the specialist group within Transport Command, Nos. 1 and 54 Squadrons were designated to provide the offensive element of No.38 Group). On 19 June 1961 the Iraqi Prime Minister, General Abdul Karim Kassim announced that neighbouring Kuwait was an integral part of his country. Under an existing agreement Britain sent military assistance to the small Arab kingdom, especially since Iraq might be expected to attack Kuwait around 14 July (the Iraqi National Day). On 30 June No.8's FGA.9s were flown to Bahrain in the Arabian Gulf to meet the anticipated threat, being joined there by 208 Squadron FGA.9s the next day. Ironically Iraq at this time included two squadrons of F.6s in its inventory. However, the Iraqi threat to Kuwait did not materialize and eventually the FGA.9s returned to RAF Khormaksar in Aden and to Bahrain. XG207, which first flew on 4 October 1956, operated on 54 Squadron from October 1965. From 1980 it operated on the TWU. (Ray Deacon Collection)

FGA.9 XE552, which first flew on 23 February 1956 as an F.6 and was converted to FGA.9 in 1960, was one of two refurbished Hunters that arrived on 208 Squadron on 2 November 1961. On 9 December it was one of eight Hunters that taxied out at Mombasa for a flypast for the Tanganyika Independence Day Celebration flypast, two being detailed as airborne spares. During takeoff, the No.2 in the front section had to abort due to insufficient power and swung across the runway. This baulked the No.3 of the second section who also had to abort. The first aircraft (XE643) left the runway and retracted its undercarriage, resulting in Cat.4 damage (later revised to Cat.5). Meanwhile, the second aircraft (XE552) also left the runway and narrowly avoiding the first, sank into the soft ground with no damage to the aircraft. The remaining six were able to form up and complete the flypast as planned and landed back at Mombasa to refuel. Two aircraft then left for Nairobi and four for Khormaksar. XE552 was able to fly out to Nairobi on the 10th where it joined the other two for the return trip to Khormaksar.

Above: FGA.9s XF376/Q on 8 Squadron with a 208 Squadron 'zap' on the forward fuselage and seven aircraft on 208 Squadron on the Kuwait new apron in July 1961. XF376 was first used by the A&AEE for trials from 1956 to 1957 before being returned to HSA on 8 May 1959 for conversion to FGA. Mk.9. It then served on 208 Squadron, 8 Squadron and RNAS Brawdy, from October 1976 and the TWU, 1976-77. (The Aviation Bookshop via Ray Deacon)

Opposite above: 8 Squadron armourers remove the covers from a trailer load of concrete-headed practice rockets at RAF Khormaksar in early 1963. In the background is FR.10 XE614, which began life as an F.6 and was operated on 263 Squadron until it was returned to HSA on 1 July 1960 for conversion to FR.Mk.10. It was purchased by HSA in June 1971 and converted to Singaporean FR.74B (533) being delivered on 21 February 1973. (Ray Deacon)

Opposite below: 'Taff' Jon watched by Dave Curryer at marshalling 8 Squadron FGA.9'E' at Khormaksar in early 1963. Every ground engineer on any squadron was trained to marshal aircraft and was responsible for any mishaps to an aircraft under his control. Concentration was vital, especially so when the aircraft were armed with cannon and rocket rounds. The rocket rails, 230-gallon drop-tanks, lack of gun blast deflectors and brake-chute housing distinguished the FGA.9 from the F.6, from which every FGA.9 was converted. Internal enhancements included additional oxygen for the longer flight duration, 'air conditioning' and an Avon 207 series engine in place of the 203. (Ray Deacon)

Above: Apart from the bowser driver, a buzz of activity is evident in this view, taken on the Khormaksar pan in early 1964, as 8 Squadron ground crew set to work on turning round FGA.9 XG169. Between flights, the Hunters were turned-round, fully armed and fuelled-up in twenty minutes (the record was eight!), so good teamwork was essential. XG169 first flew on 21 August 1956 and was operated on 19 Squadron before returning to HSA in 1960 for conversion to FGA.9. The lack of squadron markings is due to the aircraft having recently returned from refurbishment in the UK. The Hunter pan at Khormaksar could hold twenty aircraft and was shared by three units at any one time; 1417 Flight plus two from 8, 43 and 208 Squadrons. (Ray Deacon)

Opposite above: Dave Stanley on 208 Squadron arming a Hunter with SNEB rockets at Sharjah on the Arabian Gulf. Since its introduction into RAF service in 1960 the FGA.9 had to rely on World War II origin rockets for effective ground attack operations until the SNEB rocket pod was cleared for operational use in 1968.

Opposite below: In May 1964 208 Squadron moved to Muharraq on a permanent basis and it became a regular guest for Armament Practice Camps (APC) using the Jeb-a-Jib range some 50 miles west along the coast from Sharjah. Heavy sooty deposits around the canon ports on FGA.9 XK140/D on 208 Squadron are evidence that its guns had been fired on several occasions. On 3 July 1979 while assigned to 2 TWU it crashed over the sea into Enard Bay, Wester Ross, 5 miles SSW of Lochiver, Scotland after loss of control while in cloud. Captain Checa, the Ecuadorian pilot, ejected safely. This was the second RAF aircraft lost while being flown by an Ecuadorian pilot following the loss of Jaguar XX759 on 1 November 1978 and Ecuadorians were subsequently not allowed to fly solo again in British aircraft. (The Aviation Bookshop, via Ray Deacon)

FR.10 GC on 1417 (FR) Flight at Khormaksar pictured in 1964 against the backdrop of Mount Shamsan, a 1,800 feet high extinct volcano. Following the reformation of 1417 Flight in March 1963, a new unit pennant was produced and applied, initially, to the forward fuselage of the unit's five FR.10s. When centralised servicing was introduced in June 1964, it was also applied to the four T.7s. A typical month saw 1417 Flight fly 63 reconnaissance missions in June 1964, which was quite an achievement considering there were only five pilots and five aircraft, with some on standby duty at up-country airfields and other normal flying and training being carried out simultaneously. 1417 Flight operated Hunters from 1 March 1963 to 1967.

FGA.9 XE623V on 43 Squadron which crashed at Khormaksar on 11 August 1964. Flying Officer Ron Burrows was flying as No. 2 in a formation led by Flight Lieutenant John Osborne. After take-off they turned to fly at low level up the coast to the north east in battle formation. At about ten miles from Khormaksar, Ron experienced an engine flame-out caused by a failed fuel pump. He immediately pulled up to 2,500 feet and turned back towards the airfield. Several attempts at re-lighting were unsuccessful and he was obliged to eject when down to 800 feet. The aircraft, XE623, crashed in the station aerial farm and was remarkably intact for a pilot-less landing. Ron suffered the usual 'Martin Baker' back but made a quick recovery and was back on flying after only three weeks. Judging by what remained of the wreck and the length of the skid across the bondu, it must have hit the ground nigh on straight and level.

Above: 23.FGA.9 XE649/R on 8/43 Squadron over terraced Aden hinterland on 24 August 1965 as seen from a 1417 Flight FR.10, F.95 nose camera. This Hunter first flew on 30 June 1956. After Aden it served at RNAS Brawdy, from October 1976 and No.1 TWU ((79 Squadron) from 1982 when on 13 May that year it suffered engine failure due to fracture of the turbine disk and the engine caught fire. The pilot, Flight Lieutenant C. Robinson, ejected at low level and was seriously injured. XE649 crashed on moors at Cwm Ystwyth 15 miles southeast of Aberystwyth, Dyfed, Wales. (Roger Wilkins)

Opposite above: When the programme of returning Hunters from the Middle East for refurbishment in the UK began in 1963, T.7, XL612 (here captured on film in 1968 during an APC detachment at Sharjah) was modified for use in hot climates and flown out to Khormaksar where it remained with 1417 Flight for the next four years. Shortly before the British withdrawal from Aden, it was reissued to 8 Squadron and it moved up to Muharraq with the unit. When T.7, XL612-2, landed at Boscombe Down on 10 August 2001, it gained the distinction of being the last Hunter to fly in RAF service. It is pictured here in ETPS markings as a static exhibit at the Kemble Air Day two months before that final flight. After a period in storage it was obtained by a private owner for restoration to flying condition at Exeter. (Ray Deacon Collection)

Opposite below: Having been used on tropical trials in Bahrain in 1958, T.7, XL566 spent the next four years on 43 Squadron at Leuchars and Nicosia before moving with the unit to Aden. In this 1967 view the T.7 is bearing the markings of 8 and 43 Squadron on either side of the roundel with the 1417 Flight flash applied to the forward fuselage. Following the British withdrawal from Aden in 1967 and the disbandment of 1417 Flight and 43 Squadron, XL566 was reallocated to 208 Squadron at Muharraq. (The Aviation Bookshop, via Ray Deacon)

Above: FGA.9 XG237 on its nose after sand had clogged up the nose door locks - a not unknown occurrence - leading to this undignified arrival. This Hunter first flew on 5 November 1956 and was operated on 66 Squadron before conversion to FGA.Mk.9 and then issued to 43 Squadron. It was purchased by HSA on 15 January 1968 and converted to Jordanian FGA.Mk.73A (828) for delivery on 22 July 1969.

Opposite above: The extended line at Muharraq in August 1970 with a mix of 8 and 208 Squadron FGA.9s and T.7s. The pan at Bahrain could only hold ten Hunters but as the usual detachment comprised only eight FGA.9s and the occasional T.7, the far end was given over to two 13 Squadron Canberra PR.9s on six-week rotating detachments from Cyprus. (Ken Parry via Ray Deacon)

Opposite below: Hunter line up with FR.10 XJ714 nearest the camera at Sharjah in August 1970. XJ714 first flew on 13 February 1957 and was used in tropical trials in June at Idris. The Aden Protectorate with the Middle East Air Force was the major theatre in which the Mark 9 saw consistent action in RAF service. Here it remained until the end of 1971, when 8 Squadron disbanded as the last unit to operate the Hunter in front line service. XJ714 was purchased by HSA on 29 June 1971 and converted to Singaporean FR.Mk.74B, being delivery to that country on 17 January 1973. (Ken Parry via Ray Deacon)

Above: A FGA.9 on 20 Squadron at Tengah, Singapore. 20 Squadron's Hunters were often called upon to attack targets in the Malay and Borneo jungles in support of ground forces during the troubles.

Opposite above: 20 Squadron was required to send some of its aircraft and personnel to Chiang Mei, in northwest Thailand, during May to November 1962 in response to the alleged presence of Laotian forces in that country. To spread the experience and share the workload, 20 Squadron pilots were rotated between Thailand and Tengah every three weeks. The Chieng Mai Open day on 18 August 1962 (pictured) featured a five ship team led by Squadron Leader R. A. Calvert the CO and individual aeros by Flight Lieutenant Shields.

Opposite below: FGA.9s XJ683/F and XJ690/G on 20 Squadron in 1965. 20 Squadron was disbanded in February 1970, holding a joint ceremony with 45 Squadron. Both units had six aircraft in the combined flypast. XJ683 was built at Kingston as an F.6 and first flew on 7 February 1957 before being delivered to the RAF on 29 March that year. It first served on 93 Squadron and later, after conversion to FGA.9 in 1960 by HSA, on 43 Squadron. XJ690, which first flew on 12 February 1957, was converted to FGA.9 by HSA in 1964, being delivered to 20 Squadron on 31 March 1965. It returned to the UK on 19 February 1970, being sold to HSA in February 1976 for possible resale but instead the aircraft was scrapped, with only its nose section surviving and it now forms part of the Hunter displayed on a pole at Bournemouth Airport. (Richard Wilson)

FGA.9 XK142 on 28 Squadron outside the haeco hangar at Kai Tak, Hong Kong on 7 June 1967. This Hunter first flew on 8 April 1957 and was issued to 74 Squadron before returning to HSA on 28 November 1960 for conversion to FGA.9. It was delivered to 20 Squadron on 7 September 1961. Purchased by HSAQ on 5 May 1971, it was converted to Singaporean FR.Mk.74B, being delivered to Singapore on 18 August 1970. (metricbolt)

CHAPTER 4

End of Empire

In 1960-61 one by one the Hunter squadrons in the UK disbanded and they were largely re-equipped with the English Electric F.1 Lightning supersonic fighter. By April 1961 only five Hunter squadrons remained in Fighter Command and in 1963 the last two F.6 squadrons began re-equipping with the Lightning F.2. It would seem that the Hunter had had its day but Hawkers had long been aware of its potential as a very successful ground attack aircraft and they were rewarded in 1959 when it replaced the de Havilland Venom FB.4 in the close support or ground attack role in the Middle East after competitive evaluation trials held in Aden in 1958. At first the contest was seen as being between the Hunting-Percival Jet Provost and the Folland Gnat, both in use as RAF training aircraft, but the Hunter F.6 was added to the contest and easily outclassed its competitors. In 1958 Hawkers received an order to convert forty F.6s to the new FGA.9 standard. In the first instance, conversion of thirty-six F.Mk.6 airframes was carried out by RAF and Hawker teams at Horsham St. Faith (now Norwich Airport). This batch was fitted with a lower rated Rolls Royce Avon 203 and having only partial modification to Mk.9 standard was termed 'Interim Mark 9'. Five follow-on contracts would bring the total number of conversions from Mk.6 to M.9 to 128, culminating with a final batch of nine at 5 MU at Kemble in 1965.

The first FGA.9 (XG135) flew on 3 July 1959 powered by a non-surge Avon 207 and later most FGA.9s were progressively re-engined with the Avon 207. Each aircraft was fitted with a tail parachute, increased cockpit ventilation and refrigeration and increased pilot's oxygen supply. The devastating fire-power available from the four 30 mm nose-mounted cannon was retained and a strengthened wing enabled the FGA.9 to carry a multitude of stores. The inner pylon could carry a 230-gallon drop tank (with an extra strut for support), two 25 lb practices bombs, one 500 lb or 1,000 lb bomb, six '3-inch drainpipe' rockets (which dated back to WW2) or a battery carrying 24 or 37 two-inch bombs. The outer pylon could be replaced by four Mk.12 rocket rails, each of which could carry three or four of the 3-inch rockets, which in 1967 were replaced by the French 68mm SNEB (Société nouvelle des établissements Edgar Brandt) rocket.

The RAF now had one the most potent ground attack fighters in its history and it was to put it to good use. Deliveries to the RAF began in October 1959 when twelve FGA.Mk.9s entered service on 8 Squadron who began operating them at RAF Khormaksar in January 1960. These were followed in March by 208 Squadron, which in June 1960 flew to Nairobi, Kenya and began operating from Eastleigh. At Leuchars, 43 Squadron received the FGA.9 and then took the aircraft to Cyprus in June 1961. At Tengah, Singapore 20 Squadron began using the FGA.9 during the Indonesian crisis of the mid 1960s. At Stradishall Nos.1 and 54 Squadrons began received FGA.9s in January and March 1962 respectively. As Kenya was to gain independence from Britain, 208 Squadron moved to Khormaksar during 1962. President Abdul Nasser of Egypt attempted to remove the British from Aden using armed insurgents in the neighbouring state of Yemen. A mountainous area known as the Radfan, twenty miles long by fifteen miles wide, 35 miles north of Aden, was the main stronghold of the Yemeni-backed insurgents. The FGA.9s and a few Shackletons carried out leaflet dropping missions, followed by bombing strikes against the insurgents in the Radfan. On 1 March 1963 43 Squadron, which had converted to the FGA.9 in Cyprus, moved to Khormaksar. During early 1964 an increased number of hit and run raids by Yemeni aircraft on villages close to the Aden border culminated in an attack by an armed helicopter and two MiG fighters on a village and a frontier guard post. The RAF was ordered to attack Yemeni insurgents who had gained control of a fort at Harib. Hunters dropped leaflets to warn the civilian population before beginning their attack on 28 March, which was followed under cover of darkness by a paradrop by 22 SAS. At daybreak on the 29th the SAS came under heavy fire and before long, they were surrounded by three times the expected numbers of enemy tribesmen, armed with mortars and machine-guns. Eighteen Hunter sorties were flown and 127 three-inch rockets and over 7,000 rounds of 30mm cannon were fired on the rebels. The battle raged for 30 hours and two British troopers were killed. British ground forces supported by the FGA.9s later harried and hunted down the rebels. Non-stop attacks were made during May and into June, 43 Squadron alone flying more than 150 sorties and firing 1,000 rockets and 50,000 rounds of ammunition. On 18 November 1964, following a series of rocket and cannon strafing attacks by the Hunters, the last remaining dissident tribe capitulated. Fighting continued in Aden and the Hunters were used until Britain withdrew in 1967. 43 Squadron flew its last ground-attack sorties on 9 November before being disbanded as a Hunter squadron. Hunters on Nos. 8 and 208 Squadrons, which formed the Offensive Support Wing at Muharraq in Bahrain, remained until 1971 when both squadrons were disbanded.

Four FGA.9s on 28 Squadron were stationed at Kai Tak in Hong Kong from May 1962 until 2 January 1967 when it was disbanded. On 28 December 1962 Flight Lieutenant D. G. Chrichton was killed flying XE535, which flew into the Northern

Slopes of Lion Rock Ridge, two miles NNW of Kai Tak, twelve minutes after takeoff. The crash site was about 200 feet below the top of the ridge and was a hole in the mountainside surrounded by various bits of metal. A Corporal airframe fitter had previous Hunter experience and his aim was to find the flapjacks and tail plane actuator. Others just cleaned up the mess and it was bagged up and sent down to base by helicopter. The flapjacks were eventually found and they were in the extended position while the tail plane actuator was found fully nose up. Having been doing aerobatics prior to the accident, if the flaps were inadvertently left down, the faster the aircraft went it would eventually run out of nose up trim with the inevitable consequences. This turned out to be the case and was the reason put down by the board of enquiry as the cause of the accident. Just over two weeks earlier, on 10 December, Crichton belly landed another 28 Squadron Hunter at RAF Kai Tak. On that occasion neither the aircraft, or the pilot sustained any serious or lasting damage. 28 Squadron was reformed on 1 March 1968 at Kai Tak from a detachment of 103 Squadron operating Westland Whirlwind HC 10s.

British Forces in Singapore and Malaysia as part of the South East Asia Treaty Organisation (SEATO) included sixteen FGA.9s on 20 Squadron at Tengah, Singapore, which provided Day Fighter/Ground Attack for the whole theatre. Indonesia had a policy of 'Confrontation' (not all-out war) against the new Malaysian Federation and the SEATO air component was responsible for countering Indonesian Air Force incursions. Although the IAF comprised mostly obsolete F-51 Mustangs and B-25 Mitchell bombers, it was equipped with a number of Soviet fighter and bomber aircraft. (A Hunter and a MiG-17 actually chased each other around the sky on one occasion although no shots were fired). On 10 December 1962 four Hunters were deployed to Labuan, Brunei, 750 miles from Tengah due to the sudden and violent opposition directed against the Sultan of Brunei to the imminent formation of Malaysia, which would comprise Malaya, Brunei, Sabah and Sarawak. Whilst deployed the Hunters carried out numerous missions at low-level to intimidate those opposed to the political changes. On only one mission was one aircraft was permitted to fire its cannon but not at people but solely to intimidate. During the Brunei Revolt in 1962, the RAF deployed Hunters and Gloster Javelins over Brunei to provide support for British ground forces; Hunters launched both dummy and real strafing runs on ground targets to intimidate and pin down rebels. In one event, several Bruneian and expatriate hostages were due to be executed by rebels. Hunter aircraft flew over Limbang while Royal Marines from 42 Commando rescued the hostages in a fierce battle. In the following years of the Borneo Confrontation, Hunters were deployed along with other RAF aircraft in Borneo and Malaya. The rapid deployment of British forces was successful and the Hunters were cleared to return to Tengah on Christmas Day 1962.

In September 1963 the Borneo Confrontation began and a greater RAF and RAAF presence ensued when Indonesian backed guerrillas began infiltrating the Federation of Malaysia, which came into being on 16 September 1963. The British Embassy in Jakarta was burnt down as part of the protests. Soon afterwards there were small-scale penetrations into Sabah and Sarawak by Indonesian forces. Indonesian propaganda flights over North Borneo increased. 20 Squadron's first involvement was to be ordered to send aircraft to Labuan after Indonesian aircraft had been seen close to or over non-Indonesian territory. As the Hunters could not arrive at Labuan in less than ninety minutes, on 20 February 1964 four FGA.9s on 20 Squadron each detached to Labuan and Kuching. They flew surveillance and CAP in the ADIZ (Air Defence Identification Zone) encompassing North Borneo and Sarawak. In August-September Indonesian paratroops landed in force in Western Malaysia and the FGA.9s, each armed with sixteen 3-inch RPs fitted with semi-armour-piercing warheads flew rocket and cannon firing strikes. Results were unknown as 1km squares of jungle were attacked with no particular targets in sight but by the end of September almost all the Indonesian troops had either been killed or captured. Thereafter, Indonesian incursions in Malaysia were smaller and more sporadic.

Due to political constraints, offensive operations were controlled to the extent that the only weapons that were allowed to be used, when authorised, were cannons, rockets and rocket pods. This meant that only Hunters and Canberra bombers were involved. The Hunters opened fire on at least two occasions in West Malaysia. On 23 December 1964 a group of Indonesian personnel landed on the southern coast of eastern Johor and 20 Squadron and 45 Squadron's Canberra B.15s mounted strikes in response. The last such mission took place on the night of 30/31 May 1965 when some Indonesian troops landed east of Changi and quickly gained a foothold in an old WW2 Japanese fortification to await further reinforcements. Four FGA.9s directed by a FAC (Forward Air Controller), made rocket and cannon strafing attacks to dislodge them. Thirteen infiltrators were captured and the rest captured or killed later. On 1 September two B-25 Mitchells were strafed and when a Whirlwind helicopter was shot down four extra Hunters were sent to Sarawak. There were no occasions when Hunters opened fire over Eastern Malaysia, this being in part due to the difficult terrain and the fact that the border incursions by the Indonesians were limited. From October 1965 RAAF Sabres started to take over border patrol and escort duty from the Hunters. The unofficial war largely fizzled out and the Confrontation finally ended on 11 August 1966 and 20 Squadron could resume peacetime flying. The number of Hunters on strength increased due to the disbandment of 28 Squadron in January 1967. 20 Squadron remained at RAF Tengah until February 1970.

1 and 54 Squadrons which were equipped with FGA.9s formed the RAF contribution to the Allied Command Europe Mobile Forces, dedicated to the rapid reinforcement of the NATO flanks. Yet early in 1963 54 Squadron FGA.9s carried out border patrol duties along the Yemen border until relieved by 43 Squadron's FGA.9s. In August 1 and 54 Squadrons moved to West Raynham, Norfolk where they participated in air defence and reinforcement exercises in the Mediterranean and West Germany. When General Franco applied political pressure against Gibraltar, they increased the RAF presence at the Rock with three and four week detachments. The formation of RAF Strike Command on 30 April 1968 left the two NATO mobile FGA.9 squadrons as the tactical support and strike force. In July 1969 1 Squadron left for Wittering to begin conversion onto the Harrier and 54 Squadron reformed as a Phantom squadron that September. The Hunters on 8 Squadron, which had returned from the Gulf in 1971, were transferred to a number of training unit and the Squadron finally disbanded in 1980. In June 1972 it was announced that two fully operational DF/GA (Day Fighter/Ground Attack) squadrons equipped with Hunters would be formed to train the new generation of fighter pilots for the Phantom, Lightning and Harrier squadrons. After September 1974 a dedicated training school, the Tactical Weapons Unit (TWU) was established at RAF Brawdy, Pembrokeshire and on 26 July 1976, Nos. 45 and 58 Squadrons were disbanded. At its peak, TWU operated about seventy Hunters in four 'shadow squadrons', which, in time of crisis, would have become first-line squadrons. In 1978 the TWU was split into two, Brawdy becoming a Hawk station. All the Hunters moved to 2 TWU at Lossiemouth, Scotland and in 1980 it too changed to Hawks.

The last Hunters in RAF service were the ex RAF and FAA two-seaters of 237 OCU at Honington, Suffolk, which had been established in 1971 to provide dual-control facilities for RAF pilots who were to convert to the HS Buccaneer S.2. The two-seat Hunters provided an Integrated Flight Instrumentation System (IFIS) as a link between the Hawk advanced trainer and the operational Buccaneers at RAF Honington. The last operational RAF T.Mk.7s were withdrawn from use with 237 OCU in March 1994. In December the T.Mk.8s and GA.Mk.11s from FRADU at Yeovilton followed them. Many were obtained by individuals and organizations in the UK and even in countries where the aircraft never operated such as the USA, Brazil, New Zealand and South Africa.

Above: FGA.9 XF442 at the 19 Squadron Lightning F.2 station at RAF Leconfield, Yorkshire in September 1965. (Behind is Douglas C-54A-15-DC G-ASOG of Air Ferry Ltd, which was being used to help move the Lightning squadron to its new home at RAF Gütersloh in Germany. G-ASOG crashed 5km short of Frankfurt Airport on 21 January 1967). XF442 was built at Baginton as an F.6 and it served originally with 247 and 43 Squadrons before being returned to HSA on 1 June 1959 for conversion to FGA.9. It was flown for the first time in its new mark by Flight Lieutenant Tilak on 10 March 1960 and in 1962 was used for air firing trials with rocket projectiles. On 5 April 1968 Flight Lieutenant Alan Pollock on 1 Squadron, flying F.6 XF442 'H-Hotel' back to West Raynham from RAF Tangmere, flew across London and proceeded to put the power on as he passed the Houses of Parliament where a debate was in progress. Circling three times he levelled out over the Thames and rocked his wings in salute to the RAF Memorial and then approached Tower Bridge downstream at over 300 mph in an adverse bomb run before flying through the 110 feet deep × 200 feet wide gap framed by its towers and bascules! Pollock subsequently received a medical discharge from the service. In 1971 XF442 joined 8 Squadron, moving to 2 TWU in 1980. (John Hale)

Opposite above: On 15 May 1959 Hawkers decided to build a company-owned and sponsored demonstration two-seat aircraft by reusing major components from damaged and derelict Hunters. IF-19, a Belgian F.6 that had suffered a serious landing accident after only 24 flying hours, became the basis of the new aircraft. Its undamaged centre and rear fuselage with tailplane and elevators were used together with an Avon 203 engine and gearbox from Armstrong Whitworth-built F.6 XF378 after it had been cannibalised following a fuselage fire, the wings, fin and rudder from Belgian F.6 IF-67 and a two-seat Indian Mk 66 nose used as a ground display unit for the 1959 Paris Air Show. The orange and white G-APUX ('Gappux', as it affectionately became known), was first flown on 12 August 1959 by Bill Bedford, who produced a sensational public debut at that year's Farnborough Show with a series of twelve turns of an inverted spin, trailing smoke for display purposes. He repeated the feat at Farnborough in 1960. 'Gappux' was painted in military livery and from May 1963 to 1965 and was used for training purposes in Iraq, Lebanon and Jordan. In 1967 G-APUX was refurbished and acquired by Chile as a T.72, being delivered as J-718 on 9 August. It is now a static exhibit at the Chile National Aviation Museum. (Peter Amos via Ray Deacon)

Opposite below: F.6 XG172, which first flew on 27 August 1956 and was first issued to 19 Squadron. It later served on 263 Squadron, 229 OCU/63 Squadron (as '36', pictured), in 1967 and was transferred to the FAA at RNAS Brawdy in October 1976. It operated on 1 TWU from 1979.

T.7 XL586 with Flight Lieutenant Jim Vigor and his student Flying Officer Martin Bee at RAF Chivenor. This Hunter first flew on 27 June 1958 and was delivered to 229 OCU as 'ES-90' that August. It went on to serve on the IRS and, from November 1976, RNAS Brawdy. This Hunter can now to be found at Action Park in Wickford, Essex was built and first flown in 1958 it served with 1 TWU, 2 TWU and 229 OCU RAF at bases such as Brawdy and Lossiemouth, until being retired and entering storage at Shawbury in 1991. It passed through Witham Special Vehicles and Everett Aero before arriving at Delta Jets at Kemble in April 1998 - latterly as a gate guard - before being roaded to Riverside MOT Centre in Melksham, Wiltshire in August 2009. Whilst at Kemble it gained the rear fuselage and wings from XL578. The move south to Essex was in May 2011 and the aircraft may be mounted on a pole at some point in the future.

F.6 XF375 of ETPS, based at Farnborough, flown by Flight Lieutenant Graham Williams in 1966. During 1956-7 the Ministry of Supply and Armstrong Whitworth at Wymeswold and Bitteswell used this Hunter before it joined the English Electric Co. at Warton in January 1959. It joined the ETPS on 23 April 1963, moving to RAE in 1976. (Richard Wilson)

Above: F.6 XG131 on 229 OCU at Chivenor on 23 August 1969. This Hunter first flew on 16 August 1956 and trialled wing-tip tanks for HAL before being delivered to 5 MU on 10 October 1956. It went on to serve on 14 Squadron before joining the OCU.

Opposite above: T.7 XF310/T on 58 Squadron at Wittering in 1973. Another conversion from and F.4 to T.7, but not until after XF310 had participated in the Fairey Fireflash missile trials. The DH Firestreak was adopted instead and the aircraft declared surplus to requirements. XF310 then saw several years' service as an RAF trainer before being passed to the Royal Navy in 1982. Withdrawn in 1993 it was sold at auction to Skywise Aviation in Tasmania, shipped to Australia in 1997 and is currently located in Melbourne. (Ray Deacon collection)

Opposite below: T.7 XL621 first flew on 9 January 1959 and was delivered to 5 MU that February and was then issued to the Gütersloh Station Flight in August 1959. It went on to serve on the Jever Station Flight from April 1961 and 4 FTS (as '87') from 1978. (Richard Vandervord)

57

Above: FRADU GA.11 (XF977/735) on the Tain ranges, flown by Jonathon Whaley in the early 1970s. Built by Hawker Aircraft (Blackpool) Ltd as an F.4, it was issued to 118 Squadron at RAF Jever in West Germany, later seeing service with the RAF Sylt Station Flight before it was returned to the UK in 1962 for storage. Acquired by the Royal Navy and converted to GA.11 specification at Kingston-upon-Thames, XF977 was accepted into the Fleet Air Arm (FAA) at RNAS Lossiemouth on 2 October 1962, joining 764 NAS (Naval Air Squadron) at Lossiemouth on 10 October 1962 as '695'. The FRADU Hunters were unique in being the only Royal Navy aircraft that used the SNEB rockets, as they were land-based.

Opposite above: F.4 XE597 at No.1 School of Technical Training at RAF Halton in 1971. This Hunter first flew on 16 April 1956 and was issued to 63 Squadron. On 6 May 1969 it returned to HSA for conversion to FGA.Mk.9 and re-issued to 208 Squadron. It later served on 1 Squadron (which operated Hunters from 1955 until 1969) before being transferred to the FAA, at RNAS Brawdy, in October 1966 and was subsequently used by Nos.1 and 2 TWUs (here painted in 1 TWU/79 shadow Squadron when stationed at RAF Brawdy) during 1978-80. (Trevor Bartlett)

Opposite below: XF426/12 at RAF Chivenor in July 1971. Having been built as an F.6 in 1956 it saw little service with the RAF before it was returned to HSA in 1960 for conversion to FR.10 and was later presented to Jordan ('853'), being passed to Oman in 1976.

FR.10 XE626 on 79 Squadron, 229 OCU at Chivenor on 7 August 1971. It returned to HSA on 28 September 1959 for conversion to Hunter FR.10 and was delivered to 4 Squadron on 2 December 1960. HSA purchased the aircraft on 22 August 1972 and converted it to Kenyan FGA.Mk.80 ('803'). It was delivered to that country on 24 June 1974.

FGA.9 XK137/D on 45 'Flying Camels' Squadron airborne from Wittering in December 1972. This Kingston-built F.6 was flown for the first time on 11 March 1957 by Duncan Simpson and was delivered to the RAF on 8 May 1957. It served on 20 Squadron before returning to Hawkers on 2 January 1961 for conversion to FGA.9. It then served on 43 Squadron before joining the 'Flying Camels' in 1965. It was one of the attrition replacement Hunters received by Chile, on 22 May 1982 and was coded J 745. (via Group Captain Hastings)

Above: FGA.9 XF430/N on the HCU at RAF Wittering in 1973. This aircraft returned to HSA in 1964 for the conversion from F.6 and was delivered on 9 July 1965. It was purchased by HSA on 16 January 1975 and converted to Lebanese FGA.Mk.70A (L.283), being delivered on 17 May 1977. (Ray Deacon Collection)

Opposite above: FGA.9 and Harrier GR.1 aircraft from RAF Wittering in 1973. (Richard Wilson)

Opposite below: Originally built as an F.6, XF419 (pictured on 58 Squadron at RAF Wittering in 1973) after conversion to FGA.9 it operated on 1 Squadron and, from 1983, 1 TWU. (Ray Deacon Collection)

Above: FGA.9 XG154 which began life as a F.6, serving on 66 Squadron until 1960 when it returned to HSA for conversion. It then went on to serve on Nos.8 and 43 Squadrons before transferring in October 1976, to the FAA and to RNAS Brawdy and then, in 1977, to 1 TWU.

Opposite: In July 1975 four GA.11s flown by civilian pilots of Airwork Services and based at RNAS Yeovilton (otherwise known as HMS *Heron*) formed the 'Blue Herons' aerobatic team, believed to be the first aerobatic team in the world in which civilian pilots flew military jet fighter aircraft. (Richard Wilson)

In June 1962 T.8M XL580, seen here in 1976, became the 'Admiral's Barge' when it was allocated to 764 Squadron FOFT (Flag Officer Flying Training) at RNAS Yeovilton. Note the admiral's pennant painted on the nose and the white surround applied to the national insignia. XL580 first flew on 30 May 1958 and in June 1980 became one of three T.8s (the other two were XL602 and XL603) converted to T.8M by BAe to be used by 899 Squadron to acquaint Sea Harrier FRS.1 pilots under training with Ferranti Blue Fox radar equipment. Note the admiral's pennant painted on the nose and the white surround applied to the national insignia. (HAL)

T.12 XE531 of the RAE at Greenham Common on 2 August 1976. This Kingston-built F.6 was flown for the first time on 9 January 1956 by Hugh Merewether and was used by the Ministry of Supply in tropical trials before returning to Hawkers in 1959 for conversion to FGA.9 standard. When in 1962 Hawker Siddeley received an order from the Ministry of Supply for a two-seat Hunter with a 200-series Avon to carry out avionics trials for the BAC TSR.2, XE531 was refurbished to two-seat configuration and fitted with a Specto Avionics head-up display (HUD) and a vertical nose camera. In 1963 XE531 became the only Hunter Mk.12 in existence, though others were expected to follow to train operational TSR.2 aircrew. Before this could happen, however, the TSR.2 project was cancelled in 1965. XE531 was retained by the RAE as a trials aircraft at Farnborough and Thurleigh (Bedford) for development work on the Harrier, during which time it operated with an early 'fly by wire' system. XE531 crashed on take-off at Farnborough on 17 March 1983. (Adrian Balch)

Above: T.7 XL573/WC in flight. This Hunter first flew on 27 May 1958 and was issued to 229 OCU as 'ES-89' before going to RNAS Brawdy in October 1976 and later serving on 1 TWU ('83') from 1979.

Opposite above: T.7 XL566 on 4 FTS at RAF Valley on 18 August 1979.

Opposite below: With high attrition rates being experienced on the Gnat at Valley in the late 1960s and with Gnat production having ceased, the decision was taken to fill the void with Hunter Mks. 6 and 7. They entered service in camouflage (F.6) and grey with red stripes (T.7) in 1967 but received this attractive red and white colour scheme a few years later, coincident with the plating over of the gun ports. XG274 first flew on 15 November 1956 and was delivered to 5 MU on 3 January 1957, before serving on Nos. 14 and 66 Squadrons and 229 OCU and finally, 4 FTS, from 1976. It is a fine example of a 4 FTS Hunter of the period and is seen on the pan at Valley in the early 1970s. (HSA)

T.7 XL600, pictured on the pan at RAF Laarbruch in 1980 still in its former 4 FTS colour scheme when assigned to the airfield's Station Flight, first flew on 7 October 1958 and was delivered to 65 Squadron on 14 November that same year. It then operated on the Wattisham Station Flight and was involved in a bizarre incident on 10 April 1963 when, during a slow roll at 8,000 feet at 370 knots the second pilot was ejected through the canopy due to his seat not being locked into position. The parachute was damaged on the aircraft and he was killed. XL600 operated on 4 FTS from 1967-76 and on 16 Squadron from 1981. Returned to the air in civilian life, G-VETA was based at Bournemouth Airport for some time and after being sold to Delta Jets was then based at Kemble until 2004, when it was acquired by Gower Jets and flown out of North Weald and Cranwell. Sold once again in 2005 to Skyblue Aviation it then changed hands again and was briefly flown by Team Viper before ending up with Midair Squadron in August 2013. It last flew on the civil registry in 2014 and was mid-way through a major inspection when Midair closed and the company's three aircraft (two Hunters and a Canberra) were put up for auction. On 28 May 2016 XL600 arrived at the Jet Aircraft Museum in London, Ontario after the Jet Aircraft Museum purchased the classic RAF trainer at auction. (Ray Deacon)

XF300 was built as a F.4 for the RAF by Hawker Aviation (Blackpool) Ltd and it was accepted by the RAF on 9 January 1956, being issued to 234 Squadron at RAF Geilenkirchen in West Germany. It later moved to RAF Brüggen and 130 Squadron. Transferred to the Royal Navy, XF300 was converted to GA.11 specification by Hawkers and was delivered to RNAS Lossiemouth on 12 February 1963, being assigned to 738 NAS (Naval Air Squadron). By 26 March 1980 XF300 had arrived at RNAS Yeovilton to join the Fleet Requirements and Air Direction Unit (FRADU) fleet, which it served until final retirement in 1995.

T.7 XX467 at Brawdy in 1983. One of only two Hunters to bear serial numbers beyond the XL range (the other being XX466/XL620), XX467 entered RAF service as XL605 in 1959, operating with UK-based units until 1966 when it was returned to HSA for conversion to T.70 standard for the Royal Saudi Air Force. Re-serialled 70-617, it was delivered in June 1966 and was used to convert pilots from piston-engined aircraft to the Lightning. Its task over and to make good losses during the Six-Day War, it was presented to the Royal Jordanian Air Force in 1968 as '836'. In 1974, in exchange for an FR.10, it returned to the UK and issued to 229 OCU with new XX467 serial number. Retired in 1983 as a ground instructional airframe, XX467 was subsequently purchased by Gary Montgomery and moved to Kemble for restoration to flying condition by Delta Jets but a change of ownership saw it move to Exeter in 2003.) XL620 first flew on 13 January 1959 and served on 66 and 74 Squadrons before being purchased by HSA on 31 March 1966. After conversion it was delivered to Saudi Arabia on 2 May 1966. Both these Hunters went on to operate on 229 OCU and 1 TWU/79 Squadron until their retirement. (Peter Hellier, via Ray Deacon)

Royal Navy GA.11s' 868 (WT744) and 861 (XE685) (shore code 'VL') in formation with FRADU Canberra T.22 WH803/856 in 1983. From 1962 forty F.4s were converted to unarmed GA.11 standard with the addition of an airfield arrestor hook and TACAN navigation system to meet an Admiralty requirement for single-seat weapons training aircraft. After the cut off of further funds, a small number of unmodified F.4s was transferred to the FAA for a limited period. XE685 was built as an F.4 at the Hawker Blackpool factory and it was delivered to the RAF on 18 July 1955. After conversion, it was delivered to the FAA on 6 May 1963, entering service on 738 NAS at RNAS Lossiemouth. WT744 was built at Kingston-upon-Thames and flew for the first time on 28 February 1955, being issued to the Air Fighting Development School (AFDS) at RAF West Raynham for training duties. It next served on 247 Squadron at RAF Odiham before conversion to GA.11 specification and FAA service on 738 NAS.

Above: F.4 XF319 at No.1 School of Technical Training at RAF Halton in 1989. This Hunter was delivered to the RAF on 25 January 1956 and was issued to 66 Squadron and later served on 112 Squadron, 2nd Tactical Air Force, in whose scheme, complete with question mark before the roundel, is seen here.

Opposite above: F.4 XF974 at No.1 School of Technical Training at RAF Halton in 1989. This Hunter was delivered to the RAF on 15 May 1956 and issued to 3 Squadron. It went on to serve on 8 Squadron, in whose colours it is painted and finally 229 OCU before becoming Ground Instructional Aircraft 7949M.

Opposite below: WV322 at Boscombe Down in 1990. Delivered as an F.4 in 1955, WV322 first flew on 8 June 1955 and it saw limited service before being returned to HAL for conversion to T.8C configuration in 1959 and it then equipped 764 NAS and later 809 NAS for Buccaneer pilot training. With the Buccaneer's retirement from FAA service, WV322 was transferred to the RAF and flown by 237 OCU, again for Buccaneer pilot training. On retirement in 1991 it became an instructional airframe at RAF Cranwell for the local ATC squadron. WV322 (G-BZSE) was sold in 2001 to Chris Perkins. Its first post-restoration flight was on 13 March 2002. (Ray Deacon)

Hunters on 237 OCU at RAF Lyneham on 2 August 1991, the last Hunters in RAF service. 237 OCU had been established in 1971 for RAF pilots who were to convert to the Blackburn Buccaneer S.2, the two-seat Hunters providing an Integrated Flight Instrumentation System (IFIS) as a link between the Hawk advanced trainer and the operational Buccaneers at RAF Honington. (Adrian Batch)

T.8M XL719 wearing the famous 'Bunch with the Punch' markings of 899 Squadron, Royal Navy. Note the AIM-91 Sidewinder missile simulator on the outboard wing pylon. The T.8 two-seat trainer for the Royal Navy. was fitted with an arrestor hook for use on RN airfields but otherwise similar to the T.7. Ten were built new and 18 were conversions from F.4s. Four T.8Bs had TACAN radio-navigation system and IFIS fitted and cannon and ranging radar removed and were used by the Royal Navy as a Blackburn Buccaneer conversion training aircraft. The Eleven T.8C had the TACAN fit while the T.8M was fitted with the Sea Harrier's 'Blue Fox' radar, used by the Royal Navy to train Sea Harrier pilots. (Author)

CHAPTER 5

Overseas Customers

In 1954 the Swedes arrived in Britain to evaluate the F.4 to replace the J 28B Vampire and Saab J 29 'Flygande Tunnan' ('Flying Barrel') in two wings in the Svenska Flygvapnet or Swedish Air Force, since the J 35B Draken would not enter service until the 1960s. Among the suitable contenders were alternatives were the Hunter, Vickers Supermarine Swift and Dassault Mystère. The Swift at first the favoured choice, but on 29 June Sweden signed an order for 120 new-build F.4s as F.50s (but no two-seat aircraft) in what was the first export deal for the Hunter. The first Mk.50 made its maiden flight on 24 June 1955 and production continued until 1958. The Swedes were loaned an RAF F.4 for evaluation before delivery of their F.50s, the first being delivered on 26 August 1955. The type eventually equipped a total of four squadrons and an aerobatic team, the 'Acro-Hunters', flew the Hunter in displays for a short time in the early 1960s. Swedish F.4s featured a four-pylon wing without dogtooth leading edge extensions and these were retrofitted with cannon link collectors and muzzle blast deflectors. During the 1960s most or all J 34s were wired to carry the Sidewinder AAM built under license in Sweden on the outboard wing pylons. The two Flygvapnet wings, F 8 at Barkarby and F 18 at Tullinge (home base to Acro Hunters display team), each received sixty Hunters during 1955-57. When F 8 was disbanded and F 18 re-equipped with the Draken, in 1962 the J 34s were transferred to F 9 in Säve (the last base to use the Hunter in Sweden, now a museum) outside Gothenburg and F 10 at Ängelholm. Some were put in storage and no longer used. The F 10 Hunters were operational until 1966 then transferred to F 9 or put into storage.

Only four days after the Swedes finalized their deal for F.50s, on 3 July 1954, Denmark had signed a contract for thirty Mk.51s (F.4s) to equip Esk 724 in the (Kongelige Danske Flyvevâben). The first Mk.51 (E-401) was flown on 15 December 1955 and was delivered, together with E-402, on 30 January 1956. On 11 November 1955 WW591, a new F.4, had been flown to Denmark for evaluation and it was retained to enter service with the Royal Danish Air Force on the same day that the first two new-build aircraft arrived. In 1956 also, two T.Mk.53 aircraft (basically the same as the T.7 but not fitted with the dogtooth wing) were ordered and these were delivered in late 1958. In 1968-1969 two T.7s arrived from the Netherlands.

This gave a grand total of total of 34 Hunters, with at least 32 of them new-build, including E-430, the last Hunter built for Denmark, which was delivered on 18 August 1956. Esk 724 was eventually disbanded on 31 March 1974 and most of the nineteen surviving Hunters including the two T.Mk.53 trainers were repurchased by HSA for refurbishment and re-sale.

In May 1954 a joint licence-production arrangement was reached with Fokker-Aviolanda of the Netherlands and Avions Fairey and SABCA of Belgium for the manufacture of Hunters to replace Gloster F.8 Meteors in service; both companies each receiving a single British-built F.4 as a manufacturing pattern aircraft in March 1955. The first 48 Dutch F.4s and the first 64 Belgian F.4s were obtained with US defence-assistance funding, the F.4s entering formal service in 1956. In Belgium F.4s served with Force Aérienne Belge/Belgische Luchtmacht front-line units for about ten years. In 1958 these began to be replaced by licence-built Mk.6s which remained in service until replacement by the Lockheed F-104 Starfighter in the early 1960s. In total Fokker produced 96 F.4s and 93 F.6s for the Koninklijke Luchtmacht with SABCA and Avions Fairey building the majority of the 112 F.4s and 144 F.6s for the Force Aérienne Belge/Belgische Luchtmacht, although Fokker built some of the Belgian machines. At least one of the F.6s was used for atmospheric radiation sampling, carrying a collection pod built from an external tank. The Dutch upgraded many of the F.6s with wiring for the Sidewinder AAM, carried on the outer wing pylons. Some of twenty new build T.7s the Dutch obtained directly from Hawkers from 1955 may also have been wired for Sidewinders. The Belgians had a training arrangement with the Dutch and used Dutch T.7s. One of the T.7s was given a civil registration and painted in a bright orange, white and blue scheme and used by the Dutch Flight Research Establishment for flight medicine studies. Hunters were withdrawn in the Belgian Air Force from 1962. The Dutch F.4s were phased out in 1963 but the F.6s served until 1968, when they were replaced by the Lockheed F-104 Starfighter. When the F.6 was declared redundant, many had seldom exceeded 600 airframe hours and these Dutch and Belgian Hunters were sold back to Hawker Siddeley for refurbishment and re-sale to India and Iraq, with others to Chile, Kuwait and Lebanon.

Peru was an early customer for the Hunter, acquiring sixteen F.52s in 1956 to equip the 12th Fighter Group at Talara near the border with Ecuador. These were apparently new-build machines, but most were F.4s ordered by the RAF but not delivered to that service. The F.52s arrived in Peru by sea in April 1956 and they entered service with the Fuerza Aerea Peruana before the end of the year. The Peruvians obtained a single T.7 under the designation T.62 in 1959, with this aircraft featuring a radio compass in a blister just behind the cockpit. The Mk.62 entered service in March 1960. Peru considered acquiring F.6s in 1966 but decided to obtain the Dassault Mirage 5 instead, relegating the Hunters to the ground-support role in 1968 despite the two-pylon wing. They were replaced in this role in turn by the Sukhoi Su-22 in 1976, but eleven Hunters remained in the advanced training role after that, being finally phased out along with the T.62 trainer in 1980.

Chile had hoped to obtain 25 F-86F Sabres from the USA in the mid-1960s, but the deal fell through and instead obtained a series of initial batches of Hunters that included 28 FGA.71s (FGA.9s); six FR.71As (FR.10s); and five T.72s (T.66s); for a total of 39 Hunters. During 1966-88 Chile received fifteen single-seat ex-RAF, Dutch and Belgian Hunters as FGA.Mk.71s for the Fuerza Aèrea de Chile (FACh). In June 1973 the Liberian oil tanker *Napier* ran aground on Guamblin Island, accidentally releasing 30,000 tons of oil. After the rescue of the crew, the vessel was fired upon and set on fire by Chilean Hunters in an effort to burn the oil to avoid further environmental contamination. (The same scenario had been played out off British shores in March 1967 when RAF Hunters were among the aircraft called upon to try to disperse oil on troubled waters after the 61,000-ton super-tanker *Torrey Canyon* with a cargo capacity for 120,000 tons of crude oil struck Pollard's Rock on Seven Stones reef between the Cornish mainland and the Isles of Scilly and began leaking her entire cargo of crude oil from the Middle East). By September 1973 Chile had received thirteen more FGA.71s, six single-seat fighter-reconnaissance Mk.71As and six two-seater T.Mk.72s. During the September 1973 Chilean coup d'état, some of the Hunters were used by military officers as part of the effort to successfully overthrow the socialist president of Chile, Salvador Allende. On 10 September, coup leaders ordered the Hunters to relocate to Talcahuano in preparation. The following morning, the aircraft were used to conduct bombing missions against the presidential palace, Allende's house in Santiago and several radio stations loyal to the government. The UK had signed contracts prior to the Chilean coup d'état for delivery of a further seven Hunters, as well as performing engine overhauls and the delivery of other equipment. The British government delayed the delivery of the aircraft, along with vessels and submarines also on order; the trade unions took action to block delivery of refurbished Hunter engines at the Rolls-Royce East Kilbride plant until October 1978. In 1974 an embargo on the supply of spares to Chile was imposed and by 1978 only twenty aircraft remained serviceable. In 1982, during Britain's retaking of the Falkland Islands from Argentina, Chile apparently allowed RAF Canberras in Chilean markings to overfly Argentina and provided a number of other services to discreetly help the British forces. In return Chile received, in 1982-83, ten ex-RAF FGA.9s and two Kuwaiti T.67s, possibly by way of Oman, mostly for use as spares. The FACh was interested in acquiring new Hunters as late as 1994 but was unable to do so, so they acquired the Dassault Mirage 5 instead. After 28 years the Hunter was finally retired from service on 17 February 1995.

Rhodesia obtained twelve ex-RAF FGA.9s in the mid-1960s, the first RRAF Hunter arriving on 20 December 1960. The first Hunters arrived in memorable style in Salisbury with the biggest bang ever heard over the city. It brought a stream of protests from people in the Salisbury area. Two of the Hunters screamed about 1,000 feet over the capital at 400 mph and as a result, the newspaper offices were inundated with complaints about 'crying children, swooning ladies and comatose parrots'. By 15 May 1963 the final aircraft was delivered to 1 Squadron at RRAF Thornhill near Gwelo in the Central Highlands. When Prime Minister Ian Smith unilaterally declared independence from Britain on 11 November 1965 and the RRAF was renamed the Rhodesian Air Force (RhAF) Britain shut off spares supplies. Even so, nine of the original dozen Hunters were still flying with the Zimbabwe-Rhodesian Air Force at the end of the 1970s and a four-man formation aerobatic team gave displays in the late 1960s and early 1970s. Late in 1972 a major insurgency broke out and the Rhodesian Air Force operated against the Patriotic Front for seven years. The Hunters were reported to be involved in the Mozambican Civil War in 1977. In February 1979 Rhodesian Hunters attacked a Soviet-backed ZIPRA base in Angola, approaching from 20,000 feet and descending quietly to make 60° dive attacks with 1,000 lb 'Golf' blast bombs, which had a 3 feet rod projecting from the nose to ensure detonation above ground. Since the insurgents were generally operating from sanctuaries in neighbouring states that meant strikes across borders and in some cases Rhodesian Hunters flew over local airbases, asking the control tower politely to not send up any opposition - and adding that if anything tried to take off to intercept, it would be shot down. Of the twelve original Hunters, one was lost to a technical defect and two were lost to ground fire up to the political settlement of the conflict in 1979. Only one Hunter pilot was lost during the 'Bush War'; Air Lieutenant B. K. Gordon was killed when he was shot down on 3 October 1979 while attacking a Frelimo column near Chimolo in Mozambique Four FGA.80s and a T.81 were acquired from Kenya and after the end of the 'Bush War' and the creation of Zimbabwe in 1980 the Rhodesian Hunters remained at Thornhill as part of the AFZ. In the early hours of 25 July 1982, five Hunters were destroyed in a series of explosions in an insurgent attack on their ground base. Britain provided five replacement FGA.9s in 1983 and four more in 1987 but the exodus of many white engineers made it increasingly difficult for the Hunters to be kept serviceable. Zimbabwe's Hunters were flown in support of Laurent Kabila's loyalists during the Second Congo War in August 1998. The last Hunter in Rhodesian/AFZ service was retired in January 2002.

During the late 1960s and early 1970s the small oil states and Emirates of Abu Dhabi, Qatar and Oman also received Hunters with training often supervised by RAF personnel. The Abu Dhabi air force was formed at Sharjah with seven FGA.Mk.76s and three FR.Mk.76As converted from RAF aircraft and two T.Mk.77s converted from Dutch T.Mk.7s were delivered during 1970 and 1971. During the 1970s, Abu Dhabi obtained a fleet of Mirage 5s and relegated the Hunters to the ground-attack role. They were then finally phased out in favour of the BAE Hawk in 1983, with the surviving Hunters passed on to Somalia. Some sources claim that both T.77s were passed on to Jordan in 1975, but since at least one T.77 ended up in Somalia that seems unlikely. In Somalia, the Siad Barre regime's fleet of ageing Hunters, often piloted by former Rhodesian servicemen, carried out several bombing missions against rebel units in the late 1980s.

During 1968 Qatar ordered two FGA.Mk.78s identical to the Abu Dhabi FGA.76 and one T.Mk.79 for service in the Qatar Public Safety Forces. After refurbishment and a period in store they were delivered in December 1971, shortly after Qatar's independence from Great Britain. Based at Doha; these aircraft were painted in a desert camouflage scheme and flown by RAF pilots on detached duty. These Hunters were followed later by a further four refurbished aircraft. All the Hunters were replaced by six Dassault-Dornier Alpha Jets during the 1980s or early 1990s.

During 1970-71 sixteen refurbished ex-RAF F.6s were acquired by The Republic of Singapore as FGA.Mk.74s and FR.Mk.74As. Based at Tengah, they were used for air defence, army support and tactical reconnaissance, armed with SNEB-Matra rockets. By October 1973 22 Mk.74B single-seaters and nine T 75As and 75Bs 4s had joined them. During 1974 and 1975 Kenya became the last customer for refurbished Hunters when it acquired four ex-RAF single-seat FGA.Mk.80s and two ex-Fleet Air Arm T. Mk.81s.

India was the third largest user of the Hunter after the UK and Belgium with 252 Hunters. (The Belgian Air Force operated 256 Hunters manufactured by Fokker in Holland and assembled in Belgium). India's Hunters resulted from a request in November 1954 for Hawkers to outline specification, costs and delivery dates for 100 such aircraft. In April 1956 a delegation from India evaluated the Hunter F.4 and F.6 in the air and on the ground and in July 1957 agreed to purchase F.6 aircraft (designated Mk.56) as a part of a wider arms deal with Britain, ordering 182 Hunters in 1957, including 160 F.56s, which were F.6s with cannon muzzle blast deflectors and brake chutes; and 22 new-build T.66 trainers, with the Avon 203 engine, the more powerful engine being considered beneficial in a hot environment, allowing for greater takeoff weights. The first sixteen F.56s were actually F.6s obtained directly from RAF stocks, which were modified to F.56 standard after delivery to India. The remaining F.56s were delivered from Hawker. Initial delivery of the F.56 to India was on 11 October 1957, with the type going into squadron service at the end of the year. The first T.66s were delivered in February 1959. By the end of 1961 Indian Air Force (IAF) Hunters were up to strength, equipping seven squadrons.

Indian Hunters are believed to have participated in the Indian occupation of Goa in 1961, mostly as a show of force and they may have combated with Chinese MiG-17s during border squabbles in the early 1960s. Then came the Sino-Indian War in 1962. By this time India had assembled one of the largest air forces in Asia and the Hunter was the nation's primary and most capable interceptor. During the conflict, the Hunter demonstrated its superiority over China's Soviet-sourced MiGs and gave India a strategic advantage in the air. India's aerial superiority deterred Chinese Ilyushin Il-4 bombers from attacking targets within India.

During the Indo-Pakistani War (which began on 7 September 1965) the Hunter along with the Gnat was India's primary air defence fighter and regularly engaged in dogfights with the Pakistani F-86 Sabres and F-104 Starfighters. On the second day five Indian Air Force Hunters from one formation were shot down in as many minutes by a Pakistani F-86F-40 Sabre flown by Squadron Leader Mohammed Alam of the Pakistani Air Force. Caught by surprise, the first Hunter was shot down by a Sidewinder missile and the rest by gunfire. The aerial war saw both sides conducting thousands of sorties in a single month. Both sides claimed victory in the air war, Pakistan claimed to have destroyed 104 aircraft against its own losses of nineteen, while India claimed to have destroyed 73 enemy aircraft and lost 35 of its own. Despite the intense fighting, the conflict was effectively a stalemate. After this latest hostilities to beset these two nations, India ordered 53 refurbished Mk.56A single-seaters, which were basically FGA.9s, with 36 ordered in 1965, eleven in 1967 and six in 1968. Also, two more batches of two-seaters including twelve T.66Ds in 1968 and five T.66Es in 1973 were ordered. An unknown number of IAF Hunters were locally upgraded to FR.10 specification, with the camera nose.

At the beginning of the second Indo-Pakistani conflict of 3-17 December 1971 that resulted in the creation of the state of Bangladesh, India had six combat-ready squadrons of Hunters or 127 single-seat fighters and 28 two-seaters. In an event now known as the Battle of Longewala, six IAF Hunters stationed at Jaisalmer Air Force Base were able to halt the advance by Pakistani infantry and armoured forces on the Indian outpost of Longewala by conducting non-stop bombing raids. Hunters attacked Pakistani tanks, armoured personnel carriers and gun positions and contributed to the increasingly chaotic battlefield conditions, which ultimately led to the retreat of Pakistan's ground forces. Hunters were also used for many ground-attack missions and raids inside Pakistan's borders, such as the high-profile bombing of the Attock Oil refinery to limit Pakistani fuel supplies. This conflict cost India 22 Hunters.

Hunters began to be replaced in the air-combat role by the MiG-21 in the early 1970s but the Hunter lingered on in secondary roles, flying as advanced trainers and target tugs, a few of which were said to still be in service as late as 1999. The IAF retained the ageing fleets of Hunters and English Electric Canberra bombers until finally, in October 1978, the Indian government procured 200 Jaguars, a large portion of which were to be assembled domestically. By 1979 eighty Hunters remained in front-line service with four Strike Squadrons of the Indian Air Force and about twenty older Marks were employed on target towing duties and another 23 aircraft served on the OCU. In 1988 the 'Thunderbolts' display team received replacement aircraft and 20 Squadron converted to the newer Sukhoi Su-30MKI in 1990.

When Switzerland needed to replace its existing fleet of de Havilland Vampires comparative evaluation trials were held in 1957 in Britain with the Hunter up against the F-86D Sabre, T-33 Shooting Star, Mystère IV, FFA P-16 and the Folland Gnat. The Hunter seemed to offer the perfect choice and Hawkers were asked to perform a further evaluation in Switzerland using two machines on loan. In January 1958 Hawkers were rewarded when Switzerland ordered 100 F.Mk.58s for the Flugwaffe. To get Swiss pilots up to speed the first dozen Mk.58s were ex-RAF Mk.6s (which were returned to Britain later for update to F.58 specification) while the other 88 were new-build machines, with deliveries taking place from 3 April 1958 to 1 April 1960. The Swiss machines featured T.7-style brake chutes, Swiss-specified radios and stronger outboard stores pylons that could carry 880 lb bombs. Nose ballast had to be added to permit carriage of the heavier warload. The F.58s were assigned the air combat role, with the attack role as a major secondary mission. From 1963, about half the Swiss F.58s were wired for carriage of US-built Sidewinder AAMs on the outboard pylons. Initially, the Swiss did not obtain any two-seat Hunters but they did borrow Hawker Siddeley's T.66 demonstrator for a time.

In 1971 the Swiss decided to obtain a replacement for their de Havilland Venoms in the attack role. They evaluated the McDonnell Douglas A-4M Skyhawk, the Northrop F-5A, the Fiat G.91Y and the SAAB 105 and at first decided to obtain the LTV A-7G Corsair II but the competition concluded without any contract being awarded. Instead, the Swiss opted to buy thirty Mk.58A Hunters. A third contract for 22 F.Mk.58As was signed in 1973 for delivery during January 1974-April 1975. A fourth contract in 1974 purchased eight T.Mk.68s, the majority of the sixty Mk.58/68s being Mk.4s, some converted Mk.6s and T.Mk.7s. The F.58As were delivered in kit form and featured the Avon 207 engine instead of the Avon 203 engine used in the original F.58 batch. The older F.58s were later refitted with the Avon 207. The T.68's were armed with twin Aden cannon and were refitted with improved Martin-Baker ejection seats. Used only in the electronic countermeasures role, they carried a locally-built T-708 pod on an outboard pylon that contained an RF jammer in the front and a chaff-flare dispenser in the back. The right-hand seater controlled the countermeasures gear. The Swiss later acquired the Northrop F-5E Tiger II, most of them built under licence, which took over the air-superiority role and the Hunters were reassigned to the strike role.

Starting in 1974 the single-seat Hunters excepting a dozen aircraft that became target tugs, were fitted with the SAAB BT-9K bombsight used on Swiss Venoms. The target tugs were fitted with a locally-built tow/winch unit that was carried on an inboard stores pylon. The 'Hunter 80' programme in the early 1980s resulted in a US-built AN/APR-9 Radar Warning Receiver being installed in the nose along with AN/ALE-39 chaff-flare dispensers built into modified cannon link collector bins. The number of underwing rails for rockets was increased from 8 to 10 and adaptations were made to allow for the deployment of new munitions such as the Hunting Engineering BL755 cluster bomb. Some T.Mk.68s could be fitted with T-708 Vista ECM pods, containing several jamming devices and chaff dispensers. Another simple but effective improvement for landing the aircraft in icy conditions was the addition of a brake-parachute. Forty Hunters were configured to carry the AGM-65B Maverick electro-optic air-to-ground missile. A Hunter could typically carry a pair of AGM-65s and as many as twenty rockets in a combat mission.

By 1975, plans emerged to replace the Hunter in the air-to-air role with a more modern fighter, the Northrop F-5E Tiger II. The Hunter continued its service in the Swiss Air Force after the introduction of the F-5; becoming the primary ground attack fighter, a role it maintained for a further twenty years until Switzerland purchased 32 F/A-18 Hornets in the late 1990s. In 1990 there were still nine squadrons equipped with 130 Hunters: the 2nd at Ulrichen, 3rd at Ambri, 5th at Raron, 7th at Interlaken, 9th at Raron, 15th at St. Stephan, 20th at Mollis, 21st at Turtman, 22nd at Ulrichen and St. Stephan (with T.68s). They were almost the half of the first line (19 squadrons, 6 with F-5s and 3 with Dassault Mirage IIIS/RS), while one more aircraft was used by the experimental aircraft unit. The F.Mk.58A was phased out first, as there were problems with the wing's structure. The Flugwaffe lost the capability to carry out air-to-ground operations when the last of the Hunters were phased out of service on 16 December 1994, a year earlier than initially planned, but they were becoming too expensive to maintain after 36 years of continuous service In the course of operating the Hunter there were 32 crashes, causing the deaths of fourteen aircrew. Originally all the Swiss Hunters, except for a handful to be donated to museums or used for gate guards and the like, were scrapped in accordance with strict Swiss rules about exporting weapons but Switzerland could give them away and many ended up in private hands, which proved a cheaper option than scrapping them.

In the Middle East in 1957-1958 Iraq obtained an initial batch of fifteen F.6s from RAF stocks with American funding; the first aircraft arriving in 1958 but the revolution curtailed any further orders for some time. It was not until early in 1963 that a further 24 FGA.59s, which were converted from Belgian aircraft modified to FGA.Mk.9 standard, were ordered. These were followed in 1965-1966 by eighteen identical FGA.59As. After borrowing the Hawker trainer demonstrator for about a year, Iraq obtained five T.66s as T.69s in 1963-1965, followed by four FR.10s as 'FR.59Bs'. In all, Iraq obtained a total of 57 Hunter fighters, five Hunter trainers and four Hunter fighter-reconnaissance aircraft. Iraqi Hunters fought against Israel in both the 'Six-Day War' in 1967 and the 1973 Yom Kippur War, serving in both air-to-air and ground-support roles. The Israelis claimed a number of kills on Iraqi Hunters during these conflicts, while Iraqi Hunters claimed a number of kills on Israeli aircraft. At the beginning of the 'Six-Day War' the Iraqi Air Force had on strength 64 single-seat Hunters and four two-seaters. Iraqi Hunters saw action against the Israelis during the first phase of Operation 'Moked' ('Focus') in 1967 while defending H-3 airfield in Iraq. Some aerial kills against the IDF were recorded during this attack; in this instance by a Pakistani pilot that was training Iraqi pilots at the time. Jordanian pilots, whose Hunters were mostly shot up on the ground by the Israelis, flew Iraqi Hunters during the Six-Day War and other foreign pilots flew Iraqi Hunters during both conflicts. During the Six-Day War Iraqi Hunters usually operated from bases in Egypt and Syria. While flying a Hunter from Iraqi Airbase H3, Flight Lieutenant Saiful Azama of the Pakistan Air Force, who had been on exchange with the Jordanian Air Force when the war broke out, claimed three Israeli jets including a Sud Aviation Vautour and a Mirage IIICJ. In June 1972 the Hunters on strength with the IAF amounted to 35 single-seaters and three two-seaters. These aircraft were scheduled for replacement when in October 1973 the Yom Kippur War began. The Iraqi Hunters joined Syrian MiG-2 is flying top cover over the Northern Front while Sukhoi Su-7s carried out their ground attack strikes. The Iraqi Hunter pilots tended to avoid combat with Israeli Phantoms but frequently engaged A-4 Skyhawks and Super Mystères. Seven Iraqi Hunters were lost during this war but they claimed about twelve Israeli aircraft destroyed between 12-24 October. Iraqi Hunters were gradually phased out of service during the 1970s in favour of the Sukhoi Su-7, but by 1979 Iraq was still flying at least thirty Hunters, some of which were used with considerable success in ground attacks against Syrian Army tanks during the Black September Crisis during the Iran-Iraq War in the 1980s, possibly dropping chemical munitions.

In 1958-59, using American funding, Lebanon received six ex-RAF Hunter F.6 Hunters, followed later by three T.66C two seaters and four FGA.Mk.70s, all converted from Belgian Mk.6s for delivery during 1965-66. Of these, five Lebanese Hunters were lost in training accidents and six more Mk.70s were ordered in 1975, again from RAF stocks. Three of the final batch were delivered in the spring of 1976 but the remainder were detained in Britain pending the outcome of the Lebanese civil war. They eventually left for the Lebanon in December 1977. One Hunter was lost on the first day of the Six-Day War and it appears that the Hunters engaged in very little combat with the Israelis. They also saw infrequent action in the Lebanese Civil War in the 1980s. In August 2007, following the Lebanon conflict it was planned to put the Hunters back into service to deal with Fatah al-Islam militants in the Nahr el-Bared camp north of Tripoli but the programme was delayed by lack of spare parts for the aircraft, such as cartridges for the Martin-Baker ejection seats. On 12 November 2008 four of the eight Hunters (one T.66C and three FGA.Mk.70s) were returned to service with 2 Squadron at Rayak AB. These last four active Hunters were withdrawn from service by the end of 2014.

The Air Force of the Hashemite Kingdom of Jordan obtained an initial batch of twelve Hunter F.6s in 1958, followed by twelve ex-RAF FGA.9s in 1962 and then eight ex-RAF F.6s refurbished to FGA.9 standard as FGA.73s. Three T.66Bs were obtained in 1960 and two FR.10s in 1960-61. One of the FR.10s was modified from an F.6 and lacked the brake chute. King Hussein of Jordan, a skilled pilot, is believed to have checked out on the single-seat Hunter and in 1964 the Royal Jordanian Air Force formed a nine-aircraft Hunter flight demonstration team called the 'Hashemite Diamond'. Jordanian Hunters claimed a number of kills against Israeli aircraft in 1964 and 1966, but almost all 21 Hunters - the entire strength of the JAF's No. 1 Squadron - including a number of Hunter FGA.9s were destroyed during the Israeli Air Force's heavy strike attack on Mafraq during the 1967 Six-Day War when Jordanian pilots flew Iraqi Hunters. Only two Hunters survived the attack and these were badly damaged. Jordan rebuilt its Hunter force after acquiring three F.6s presented by Saudi Arabia and four ex-RAF FGA.9s and two batches of refurbished Hunters, including twelve FGA.73As and three FGA.73Bs; delivered between 1968 and 1971. In 1975 Abu Dhabi loaned King Hussein its entire strength of twelve Hunters to join the nineteen surviving Jordanian aircraft, which were soon phased out in favour of the Northrop F-5E and the Cessna T-37. King Hussein presented all his ex-RAF F.6s and 31 Hunters to the Sultan of Oman in 1975.

In 1974-75 the Sultan of Oman's Air Force was expanded with several types of aircraft including, donated by Jordan, eight F.6 aircraft (most of which were used for spares), two ex-Dutch Air Force F.6s converted to T.66B aircraft, 25 FGA.73A/B fighter bombers and two FR.10 reconnaissance versions and two T.67s donated by Kuwait. However, only about fifteen Hunters from the whole fleet were in flyable condition, whilst the others were retained in storage as replacements and to provide spares for the operational aircraft. Some of the FGA.73A/Bs were upgraded (by Singapore Industries) with Tracor AN/ALE-40 chaff/flare launchers, LORAN 'towel rack' antenna and wing pylons with LAU-7/A launchers with AIM-9P Sidewinder missiles. The Hunters were flown by RAF pilots on detached duty and others by mercenaries and used operationally over Southern Yemen on cross-border operations armed with Pakistani 1,025 lb bombs and 88mm Hispano SURA rockets and 30mm Aden for strafing. Two FGA.73Bs were shot down; ex-Jordan '854', on 17 November 1975 when Jordanian pilot Mohammed Faraj ejected and ex-Jordan '851' on 27 March 1986 when Flight Lieutenant Keith Middleton was killed. Ex-Jordan '848' was hit by AA fire whilst operating over southern Yemen during the border war but recovered to Thumrait and was later scrapped. A few other Hunters were damaged but repairable. In 1979 twelve Hunters were serving with the Sultan's No. 6 Squadron at Thumrait, his Air Force's principal strike base. The few surviving Hunters were phased out in November 1993.

As part of the so-called 'Magic Carpet' arms deal with Saudi Arabia, Hawker was contracted to supply the Royal Saudi Air Force with four Mk.6s and two Mk.7s early in 1966 as a stopgap measure pending delivery of a much larger order of English Electric Lightnings. The Hunters reached Riyadh in May 1966 and they were used to form 6 Squadron RSAF at Khamis Mushayt which used them to deter incursions by Egyptian aircraft. But when Egyptian Air Force MiG-21s and 11-28s carried out a number of attacks on Saudi Arabia, the Hunters were unable to intercept any of them owing to an almost total lack of ground control and the pilots were used instead on retaliatory ground strikes. In 1969 the three remaining F.6s were given to Jordan.

Though the orders received from the Middle East for Hunters were small, they paved the way for the massive British arms deals for aircraft such as the Lightning, Hawk and the Tornado. All the refurbishment activity helped fund other projects, not least of which was the highly successful P.1127/Kestrel/Harrier series.

Above: Koninklijke Luchtmacht F.4 N-101 on 322 Squadron at Biak, Netherlands New Guinea. During the conflict with Indonesia over Dutch New Guinea (1962) the Dutch air force stationed a squadron of Hunters at Mokmer airfield. In 1958 the Netherlands sent in military reinforcements to New Guinea, including an air force detachment which was stationed on Biak. First of all, the Dutch Air Force installed two radar warning systems, one on Biak and the other on the small island of Woendi situated nearby. In 1960 the Air Force was given an assignment under the code name of 'Fidelio Plan' to organize the Commando Air Defence Dutch New Guinea consisting of twelve F.Mk.4s on 322 Squadron and two Alouette helicopters, a radar navigation system on Biak and a reserve air strip on Noemfoer. The aircraft and helicopters were transported in by the aircraft carrier *Karel Doorman*. A year later, another twelve F.Mk.6s were supplied.

Opposite above: F.6 N-276 of the Koninklijke Luchtmacht. This Hunter was purchased by HSA on 4 October 1966 and converted to Chilean FGA.Mk.71 (J-706), being delivered to that country on 7 February 1968.

Opposite below: F.6 N-219 and T.7 N-304 of the Koninklijke Luchtmacht at Soesterberg on 17 June 1967. N-219 was purchased by HSA on 30 July 1968 and converted to Qatari FGA.Mk.78 ((QA11) and was delivered on 20 December 1971. N-304 (XM117) was the first of twenty T.Mk.7s for the Dutch Air Force. It was first flown on 19 March 1958 and was delivered to Twente on 18 July that same year. It was purchased by HSWA on 6 August 1968 and converted to Abu Dhabian T.Mk.77 (712), being delivered to that country on 15 May 1970. (Johan 'Hans' A. Engels)

Above: F.Mk.4 ID-139, 7J-N of the Force Aérienne Belge (FAé)/Belgische Luchtmacht (BLu) from the initial batch of 112 undertaken by Avions Fairey in Brussels and SABCA during 1955-56, which served on Nos. 1, 7 and 9 Wings at Beauvechain, Chièvres and Bierset respectively. The F.4s operated by 1 Wing at Beauvechain were replaced by 53 Avro Canada CF-100 Mk 5 Canuck all-weather fighters Mk 5s from 1957 to 1964. (Daniel Brackx)

Opposite above: F.6 IF-75 of the Force Aérienne Belge (FAé)/Belgische Luchtmacht (BLu). This Belgian-built Hunter was purchased by HSA on 30 October 1962 and converted to Iraqi FGA.Mk.59 (587), being delivered on 14 January 1965. (Air Historical Team KLM-MRA)

Opposite below: F.6 IF-115, IS-M of the Force Aérienne Belge (FAé)/Belgische Luchtmacht (BLu). The Hunter F.6 operated with Nos.7 and 9 Wings at Chièvres and Bierset of the Belgian Air Force. No. 9 Wing was disbanded in 1960 and by 1963 the Hunter squadrons in 7 Wing had also gone. Belgium phased out the last of their Hunters in 1963, selling most of them back to Hawker Siddeley at near-scrap prices. Many were new-condition aircraft with only a handful of hours of flight time. IF-115 was purchased by HSA on 13 January 1965 and converted to Indian Mk.56A (A473), being delivered on 2 November 1966. (M. Biers et-Lavigne collection-via P. Doppagne)

In 1957, soon after the previous Acrobobs aerobatic team disbandment, their team leader, Major Robert Bladt, again formed an aerobatic team from No. 7 Fighter Wing at Chièvres flying Hunters in standard camouflage. On 12 June 1957 this new, as yet unnamed, team performed their first public display at Valenciennes, France. On 10 October 1959 at the Chièvres airshow, this team presented a formation of nine aircraft (with the lower wing skins painted in national Belgian flag colours) and along with sixteen standard F.6s. The team's future then became uncertain since some of the Air Force commanders had decided that these big formations were too expensive. Fortunately, the new Station Commander at Chièvres decided to keep the team alive, but flying only with four bright-red painted Hunters and using two more as spares. The team then finally received its name - 'Red Devils' and performed under this name for the first time in 1960. On 23 June 1963 the 'Red Devils' performed for the last time at Chièvres with Hunters. In 1965 the team was reformed but this time was equipped with seven Fouga Magister CM-170R jet trainers.

Like the Swiss, the Swedes also hangared many of their Hunters in underground caves for protection. In 1941 the Swedish Air Force began building its first underground hangar at F 9 Save, near Gothenburg in south-west Sweden. After World War II plans were drawn up for building underground hangars at every air force base that had suitable rock conditions but this proved too expensive and were reduced to hangars at certain selected air bases. A second underground hangar was built in 1947 at F 18 Tullinge which began operating in 1950. After that plans were finalized for building underground hangars capable of surviving close hits by tactical nuclear weapons. This required that these new hangars be much deeper, with 25 to 30 metres of rock cover and heavy-duty blast doors in concrete.

Above: On 29 June 1954 Sweden ordered 120 new build F.4s as F.50s (J 34) for the Svenska Flygvapnet in what was the first export order for the Hunter. The J 34s (the first, which was delivered on 26 August 1955 by Major Stenberg, pictured) earned a reputation for being robust and usable under field conditions. On the first 44 Hunters, the canopy had to be jettisoned before ejection of the Martin Baker Mk 2 seat; on the rest it was done automatically in sequence with the ejection. Finally, the seat was modified to be able to eject through the canopy. Swedish (and Danish Hunters) were not fitted with wing-leading edge extensions.

Opposite above: Royal Danish Air Force (Kongelige Danske Flyvevâben) F.Mk.51 E-427 during an exchange visit at Leeuwarden in May 1973. This Hunter was delivered to Esk 724, the only Danish squadron to operate the Hunter, on 6 July 1956. The first Mk.51 (E-401) was flown on 15 December 1955 and was delivered, together with E-402, on 30 January 1956. Today, E-401 is displayed at Flyvevâbenets Historiske Samling. (Frank Klaassen)

Opposite below: RDAF Mk.51s E-427 and E-408 during an exchange visit at Leeuwarden in May 1973. E-408 was delivered to Esk 724 at Vaerløse on 18 August 1956. E-427 was purchased by HSA on 28 February 1976 and disposed of to Brough Apprentices School. E-408 was purchased by HSA on 10 April 1976 and disposed of to RAF/RNAS Brawdy on 28 February 1978. (Frank Klaassen)

Above: Peru was an early customer for the Hunter, acquiring sixteen F.52s (XF970 pictured) in 1956 to equip the 12th Fighter Group at Talara near the border with Ecuador. After being retired from front-line service the Peruvian single-seat Hunters (and the T.62 trainer) were used in the advanced training role until 1980. (Ray Deacon Collection)

Opposite above: FR.Mk.71As of the Fuerza Aérea de Chile (FACh) in formation. J-728 (F.6 XE644) was delivered to Chile on 7 July 1971. J-740 was the only Hunter built in Chile for the Maintenance Wing, from parts rescued from IF-141, an F.6 purchased by HSA from Belgium on 23 October 1964 for conversion and delivered on 21 September 1971, which suffered a crash landing in April 1977 and mainly the wings from J-707. It was coded X-001 and in 1980 was exhibited at the International Air Fair (FIDA), being used for testing in 'Programa Aguila' before being assigned to Grupos de Aviacion No.8 at Antofagasta in northern Chile. J-734 (F.4 XF317) was a former Halton Ground Instructional Airframe) and J-732 (F.4 XF323, which was delivered to the RAF on 17 February 1956 and which served at the RAF College Manby before being purchased by HSA on 30 October 1971) was delivered to Chile on 7 September 1973.

Opposite below: In 1989 almost the entire surviving FGA.71s were given the 'Programa Aguila' ('Eagle') upgrade, implemented by the Chilean firm ENAER, featuring a locally-built Caiquin radar warning receiver with an antenna mounted on the top of the tailfin; chaff-flare dispensers and improved cockpit instrumentation and other improvements. The Hunters were also wired for Israeli 'Shafir' AAMs (pictured firing this missile).

blast
door
position

During WWII the neutral Swiss military airfields were for the first time equipped with simple semi round concrete U-43 type shelters protecting the aircraft parked underneath. Beginning in 1947 these open shelters became even better protected with steel doors thus creating the U-68 type shelter. At the start of the Cold War the Swiss Army began building retablierstollen (re-equipping caves) at airfields at Alpnach, Buochs, Meiringen, St.Stephan and Saanen with 100m long straight tunnels comparable with an autobahn tunnel making it possible to store and eventually re-arm aircraft like the Messerschmitt Bf 109. In the early 1950s the first larger excavations took place creating more space in the existing caves at Ambri, Alpnach, Buochs, Meiringen, Raron and Turtmann which enabled aircraft to be serviced and some minor repairs carried out. The first larger constructions became operational during 1951-1954. In the 1960s the retablierstollen excavations, now called cavernes, were further modernized and extended. Underground command and communication posts were constructed together with ammunition and fuel storage facilities, generator and technical rooms to keep the facility running and of course also personnel quarters. Fuel storage was located behind all tunnels allowing the caverne to sustain 22 aircraft for about ten days without the need for electricity, fuel and ammunition etc from the outside world. Six Flugzeugkaverne (aircraft cavernes), each with space for thirty or more aircraft, were constructed. Meiringen (also known as the Unterbach military airfield) is now the only airfield with fully operational cavernes. (Swiss Air Force)

Extensive lines of Hawker Hunters generally painted in standard RAF colours were common at many Swiss military airfields across the country for thirty-six years from the late 1950s until the early 1990s but exercises involving Swiss Air Force Hunters for a possible Cold War scenario where their bases had been destroyed were regularly practised. In 1991, during a major training exercise involving eight Mk.58s and eight F-5s, up to 4 kilometres of guard rails had to be removed from public roads to enable aircraft operations. Typically, Switzerland maintained about 150 Hunters in an operational flight-ready condition. (Captain Werner Naef, Swiss Air Force Retd)

Above: T.Mk.72 (XE704) J-736, one of six single-seaters plus the second P1101 trainer prototype (XJ627), which were brought to full two-seat trainer standard for the Fuerza Aèrea de Chile (FACh). J-736 was built as an F.4, being delivered to the RAF on 7 October 1955 and serving on 112 Squadron before becoming a Ground Instructional Airframe (GIA) at RAF Halton. It returned to Hawkers in January 1972 and after conversion to T.Mk.72 was delivered to Chile on 15 February 1974. The last Chilean Hunters were phased out in 1995. (Christian Marambio)

Opposite above: A pair of Swiss Hunters landing at Dübendorf in August 1990. The Swiss Hunters had some important upgrades, known as KAWEST (Kampfwertsteigerung or 'Increased Operational Performance'). In 1963 the Sidewinder missile was added to enhance the Hunter's air-to-air combat capability. Swiss Hunters featured several armament changes, such as the integration of SURA and SNORA 80mm rockets, as many as 32 rockets could be fitted on underwing rails. Operationally, Swiss Hunters could be armed with napalm bombs in addition to conventional loads. (Author)

Opposite below: Changing a gun-pack on a Swiss Hunter. In the early 1950s air-firing trials identified a need to fit a housing to collect spent cartridge cases and links that might otherwise damage the airframe. Two blister fairings, which the RAF knew as 'Sabrinas' after an unusually well-endowed young starlet, cured the problem. Swiss Hunters were said to have enlarged 'Sabrinas' for weapons training, collecting both links and cases. The rapidly replaceable gun-pack was lowered from the aircraft on three bomb hoists, the four barrels having been detached and left in the blast-tubes. When fired the pack automatically ventilated by opening a small electrically operated air-scoop in the starboard gun-bay access panel. The Hunter was armed with four electrically fired and controlled 30mm Aden cannon with 150 rounds per gun but it was found that the feed operated more reliably if the ammunition was restricted to 135 rounds per gun, which corresponded to just less than seven seconds fire. (Author)

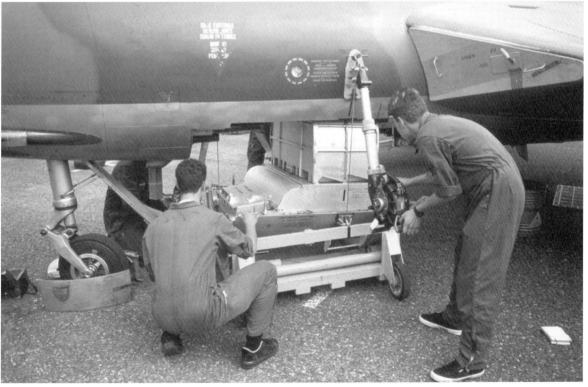

Above: Swiss Air Force F.58A, J-4105 and F.58, J-4007, practice synchronised raising of their undercarriages as they depart Dübendorf Air Base in 1981. Both are currently preserved, J-4007 in Interlaken and J-4105 in the USA. The latter is a conversion from ex-RAF F.4 XF303, which first flew in December 1955 and served on 66 Squadron before being transferred to the Fleet Air Arm as a ground instructional airframe. It returned to Hawkers in 1970 for conversion to an F.58A and was delivered to the Swiss Air Force in 1972. On retirement this Hunter was acquired by the OFMC and in 2005 it joined the Hunter Flying Club fleet at Exeter, but was later sold to Hunter Aviation, a US company. (Urs Harnisch, via Ray Deacon)

Opposite above: Swiss Air Force Patrouille de Suisse display team taking off from Greenham Common. (Author)

Opposite below: While the Flugwaffe (Swiss Air Force) operated Hunters for thirty years the national display team, the Patrouille Suisse was founded on 22 August 1964 with four Hawker Hunters, rising to five in 1970 and then six. In 1977 a smoke system was introduced. The Patrouille Suisse flew its Hunters for the last time in 1994 and transitioned to the faster and more manoeuvrable Northrop F-5E Tiger II. (Author)

Several F.58s received special colour schemes towards the end of service in the Swiss Air Force, the most striking being J-4040 or the 'Paper Plane' of Fliegerstaffel (Squadron) 15 (which disbanded in 1993) commonly known by its nickname, 'Papyrus'. The Squadron Commander, Ueli Leutert, decided to have this aircraft painted all-white and marked with the squadron and aircrew and ground crews' names in typewriter fonts and the left underwing Swiss insignia featuring a white cross modified to look like a paper aircraft, representing the unit emblem. J-4040 is preserved in airworthy condition by the Hunter Verein Obersimmental at its former base at St. Stephan and is a regular performer at air shows across Europe. (Urs Harnisch via ray Deacon)

During 1974 and 1975 Kenya became the last customer for refurbished Hunters when it acquired four ex-RAF single-seat FGA.Mk.80s (FGA.9s (XF309; XF972 and XF975 and one F.Mk.6 (XE626) and two ex-Fleet Air Arm T. Mk 81s (T.8s WT577 and XL604). One of the T.81s was later lost in an accident and the four FGA.80s were replaced by Northrop F-5s in 1979. These and the surviving T.81 were sold to Zimbabwe.

Early in 1963 24 FGA.59s converted from Belgian aircraft modified to FGA.Mk.9 standard were ordered for the Iraqi Air Force and these were followed by eighteen identical FGA.59As in 1965-1966.

Above: As part of a defence agreement between Britain and Kuwait four FGA.Mk.57 single-seaters (converted from former Belgian F.Mk 6 aircraft) and five T.Mk.67 two-seat trainers (converted from former RAF, Belgian and Dutch single-seat aircraft) were sold to Kuwait. The single-seaters were delivered between 1965 and 1966 and the two-seaters in two batches, two in 1965 and thee in 1969. The single-seat aircraft were withdrawn in 1976 when they were replaced by the A-4 Skyhawk but the two-seat Hunters continued in a training role. The single-seaters were phased out in favour of Douglas A-4 Skyhawks in 1976, but the surviving T.67s remained in service until 1980.

Opposite above: FGA.70A L-282 of the Al Quwat Al Jawiyya Al Lubnaniya (Lebanese Air Force) pictured at Dunsfold prior to delivery in 1975. L-282 was built as F.6 WW594 in 1955 and was allocated as an aerodynamic test aircraft for the DH Firestreak missile, in which capacity it flew until 1960 when it was converted to FR.10 standard for service with the RAF. Subsequently purchased by HSA, the aircraft was further converted to FGA.70A specification. (HSA)

Opposite below: The once prominent features and 'Patrouille Suisse' colour scheme of former Swiss Air Force F.58, J-4025 were removed before it was restored in Jordanian Air Force markings (712) for presentation to the Royal Jordanian Historic Flight. Here, it touches down at Kemble after participation at a UK air show in 1997, shortly before its ferry flight to Amman. (Glen Moreman via Ray Deacon)

Above: India was the third largest user of the Hunter after the UK and Belgium with 252 Hunters. The Belgian Air Force operated 256 Hunters manufactured by Fokker in Holland and assembled in Belgium. The Hunter was used by 7 Squadron 'The Battle-Axes'; 14 Squadron 'The Bulls'; 17 Squadron 'The Golden Arrows'; No.20 'The Lightnings' Squadron - the Unit also flew the Hunters in a nine-aircraft formation aerobatic team rechristened 'The Thunderbolts'; 27 Squadron 'The Flaming Arrows'; 37 Squadron 'The Black Panthers'; Operational Conversion Unit (OCU) 'The Young 'Uns' (briefly redesignated as 122 (Ad Hoc) Squadron IAF during the 1971 War) and 2 Target Tug Unit 'The Banners'. The 'Thunderbolts' flight demonstration team (pictured) was formed in 1982 as part of the IAF's Golden Jubilee. The team flew nine F.56A aircraft until disbandment in 1988. 'The Lightnings' Squadron was disbanded in 1990.

Opposite above: Six Indian Air Force Hunters of No. 2 Target Tug Flight at Kalaikunda Air Base in 1999. (The Aviation Bookshop, via Ray Deacon)

Opposite below: F-68A A484 in the markings of the final Indian Air Force Hunter unit, No.2 Target Tug Flight, the 'Banners' overshooting Kalaikunda airfield in November 1999. This former Belgian F.6 was actually built by Fokker in 1958 but saw limited service before being withdrawn and stored in 1963. Purchased by HSA a year later, it was converted to F.56A standard for the Indian Air Force and delivered in 1967. Having served with the IAF 'Thunderbirds' display team it was one of the last Hunters to fly with the IAF on the type's withdrawal in November 2001. (The Aviation Bookshop, via Ray Deacon)

One of the ex-RAF FGA.9s received from Britain for the RRAF. Rhodesia obtained twelve ex-RAF FGA.9s in the mid-1960s, the first RRAF Hunter arriving on 20 December 1960 and by 15 May 1963 the final aircraft was delivered to 1 Squadron at RRAF Thornhill near Gwelo in the Central Highlands. At least some Rhodesian Hunters were wired for carriage of the South African 'Agile Darter' AAM, another heat-seeker in a class with the Sidewinder. Rhodesian aircraft carried RPs; napalm tanks; cluster bombs filled with 'flechettes' (small metal darts); and the 1,000 lb 'Golf' bomb (a blast-fragmentation munition fitted with an extended 'daisy cutter' fuse). (RRAF)

In early 1966 a staff officer at the RhAF HQ, Squadron Leader Don Brenchley, began an initiative to give the Hunters a reconnaissance capability. Engineers on 1 Squadron modified the front end of a 100-gallon fuel tank into a camera pod by installing three F95 cameras. One camera faced forward and the other two were obliques, giving an overlapping view to port and starboard, as well as vertically under the aircraft. The camera controls were fairly basic, enabling the pilot to operate the forward camera separately as the aircraft approached the target, followed by the verticals as the aircraft passed over the target. Although this modification was fairly rudimentary, it worked well and the drop tank camera pod proved capable of providing clear overlapping photographs from low passes at 200 feet and 400+ knots. For reconnaissance sorties the 100-gallon drop tank camera pod was always carried on the port outer pylon, with a normal 100-gallon tank on the starboard pylon and 200-gallon tanks on both the inner pylons. Hunter reconnaissance sorties were usually flown from RhAF New Sarum, near Salisbury, which had a better equipped photographic section than Thornhill. The drop tank camera pod was used successfully on many sorties throughout the 'Bush War'.

Above: Having survived without a two-seat Hunter for twenty years, the RRAF took the opportunity to purchase the sole remaining Kenyan Air Force T.Mk.81 trainer in 1982. Originally one of ten new build T.8s for the Royal Navy in 1958, XL604 was purchased by HSA on 16 February 1973 and converted to T.81 standard for the KAF. With serial number 802, the delivery flight took place in the following year. Renumbered 1084 in the renamed Air Force Zimbabwe (AZF), it was pictured on the Thornhill ramp in 1997. (Ian Malcolm, via Ray Deacon)

Opposite above: Air Force of Zimbabwe (AFZ) FGA.Mk.9 ('1258') airborne in 1997.

Opposite below: Singapore Air Force FGA.Mk.74 (515) on 140 'Osprey' Squadron at Paya Lebar. This former F.6 (XJ643), which had been damaged in a collision with XG295 on 11 May 1957 was returned to HSA on 11 May 1959 and converted to FGA.Mk.9. It was purchased by HSA on 6 February 1970 for the conversion and the completed aircraft was delivered to Singapore on 24 March 1971. Ordered in 1968 with delivery starting in 1971 and completed in 1973, the RSAF operated a total of 46 Hunters (twelve FGA.74s, 26 FR.74A/Bs and eight T.75/As, excluding one T.75A which was lost in accident before delivery) from 1971 to 1992. (The Aviation Bookshop, via Ray Deacon)

Above: Retired 140 Squadron, Republic of Singapore Air Force (RSAF) FR.Mk.74B '527' outside the RSAF Museum. This ex-RAF Hunter (XF458) was converted to FR.10 and issued to 2 (FR) Squadron before it was purchased by HSA in May 1971 for the conversion to a Mark 74B, being delivered on 11 October 1972. The last Hunters in Singapore service were phased out in 1992, being replaced by the General Dynamics F-16 in the fighter role and the Northrop RF-5E TigerEye in the reconnaissance role. Only four of the Hunters were preserved as museum exhibits while the remaining 21 airworthy airframes were sold to an Australian Warbird broker, Pacific Hunter Aviation Pty, in 1995.

Opposite above: FR.Mk.60 60-602 (XE591) was one of four ex-RAF F.Mk.6s delivered to 6 Squadron at Khamis Mushayt Airbase in May 1966 as part of the 'Magic Carpet' arms deal between the United Kingdom and the Kingdom of Saudi Arabia. Although these Hunters were operational following attacks on Saudi Arabia by the Egyptian Air Force in 1967 they were not a success as interceptors as they lacked any ground control but were used for ground attack. One of the F.60s was lost and the remaining Hunters, including 60-602, were presented to Jordan in 1968. Since 1999 '60-602' has been replicated at the RSAF Museum at Riyadh by XJ634, which first flew on 3 January 1957 and served on 93 Squadron and 1 TWU before being retired to ground instructional use at Cranwell in 1981, then spending some time in storage with Everett Aero before being presented to Saudi Arabia.

Opposite below: FGA.78 QA12 (with the nose of T.79 QA13 in the foreground) at Luqa, Malta during the ferry flight to the Qatar Emiri Air Force (QEAF). Following Qatar's independence from Britain in 1971 the QEAF relied heavily on seconded RAF personnel with the aircraft maintained by Airwork Services Ltd. QA12 served in the QEAF until retirement in December 1982 and, along with the other Hunters, was based on the south-east side of Doha International Airport. The sole T.79 trainer, QA13, reportedly survives as a gate guard to the military section of Doha's airport. (ATPH)

Above: Sultan of Oman Air Force (SOAF) Mk.73B (XF426), formerly Jordanian FGA.73 (853) at Thumrait in 1975. Upon withdrawal in October 1993, this splendid aircraft was fully restored for static display and presented to the RAF Museum at Hendon on 14 October 2003 by Air Vice Marshal Yahya bin Rasheed Al-Juma. (Ray Deacon Coll)

Opposite above: Sultan of Oman Air Force (SOAF) FGA.73 '847' in the midday sun at Thumrait. It was built as F.4, XF968 and after a short period of service with the RAF and a longer period in storage, it was converted to FGA.73A standard by HSA and delivered as 847 to the Royal Jordanian Air Force (RJAF), delivery taking place in 1971. 847 was donated to the SOAF in 1975 and on retirement, became the Gate Guardian at the former RAF airfield at Salalah. 842 was returned to Jordan, to the King Hussein Air College at Mafraq Air Base. (Ray Deacon collection)

Opposite below: Ex-Jordanian T.Mk.66B ('718')/Omani '801' on 6 Squadron SOAF at Thumrait on 11 December 1986, an Armed Forces Day. Note the missile rails on the inboard weapons pylons and the two cannon as opposed to the single Aden on the RAF T.7. In September 1976 T.66B 800 (ex-Jordan '716') crashed into a ditch during a taxi run at Thumrait following a brake fire and burned when the underwing tank caught fire, killing the pilot Roger Hyde and passenger Ian 'Mac' McGrory. No ejection seats had been fitted. On 16 January 1990 T.66B '802' (ex-Jordan '810') suffered an engine flameout and Squadron Leader C. P. 'Paddy' Roberts and Mqd. Tay. Mohammed Abdul al-Baluchi ejected. (I. Hawkridge)

Above: Omani Mk.73B during a lo-lo beat up! The last Omani Hunters were withdrawn from service in 1993.

Opposite above: In 1983 Somalia is believed to have received a number of Hunters (some sources claiming six, including five FGA.76s and a T.77; and others claiming nine, including seven FGA.76s, one FR.76A and a T.77) which Abu Dhabi had presented to Jordan in 1975 to replace Hunters destroyed in the Yom Kippur War. It was reported that the Somali Hunters were flown by ex-Rhodesian Air Force pilots until the breakdown of civil order in Somalia in 1991 saw the grounding of the Somali air force. In 1993 photos were taken of several Somali Hunters (like FGA.Mk.76 CC702 pictured), showing them to be in sadly dilapidated and totally unflyable condition.

Opposite below: In August 2010 Thunder City in Cape Town shut down the operation blaming the financial climate and inconsistencies in how the South African CAA applied their regulations. The Jet squadron once operated seven Hunters, three Buccaneers, three English Electric Lightnings and one Strikemaster.